# BY THE LIGHT OF THE STAR

*An Exploration Into Creating Your Own Reality*

NICK ASHRON

Starship Pegasus Promotions
Copyright © 2006 Nick Ashron / Starship Pegasus Promotions.

This paperback edition published by
**Real2Can Books**
United Kingdom
www.real2can.com

Cover Illustration by Stu Jones
www.stujones.com

# Contents

Dedication

Acknowledgements

Foreword

By the Light of the Star

Introduction

Chapter One: Climbing Trees

Chapter Two: Chapattis and Pecan Pie

Chapter Three: Music and the Desert Sun

Chapter Four: Peace, Love and the Wild Man of Borneo

Chapter Five: Here Comes the Sun

Chapter Six: And So It Begins

Chapter Seven: The First Seeds are Sown

Chapter Eight: All that Glitters is Not Gold

Chapter Nine: All Change

Chapter Ten: Myth and Magic

Chapter Eleven: Into the Fire

Chapter Twelve: Gateways to the Stars!

Chapter Thirteen: My First Contact

Chapter Fourteen: The End?

About the Author

Recommended Reading

## *Dedication*

Dedicated to all Light-Workers and all those individuals that have inspired and supported me on my journey - my children Carly, Marc and Anna (my Web Wizard) and all those that have become my friends.

## Acknowledgments

I acknowledge with joy, honour and gratitude (both on the Earth plane and in Spirit) all the Spirit Guides, Angels, Star-Beings/Star-People, all those of the Elfin/Faery Kingdom, the Spirits of the Trees, Plants, Flowers, Rivers, Oceans, Sky, all the Animal Kingdom, Mother Earth and Divine Creator.

## *Foreword*

Since he was a young boy, Nick always had an 'inner knowing'. His journey through his lifetime has been to discover what it was that he knew!

A great part of this journey entailed discovering and knowing what is 'not' as a part of knowing what 'is' - giving him profound understandings and insights towards the meaning and purpose of his life.

It was apparent at an early age that Art and Music were going to be the tools that would provide the insights, experience and wisdoms that Nick has now come to understand.

Nick Ashron has now written an autobiographical account of his own Spiritual journey, in the hope of inspiring and empowering others on their own Spiritual journey, and to encourage them to review their own life story and discover the guidance that was and is, always there for them.

## By the Light of the Star

Although this story has an autobiographical context, it is not intended to be just a simple account of the Author's personal history. It is more to share the events and experiences that served to trigger a change and expansion in the Author's views and perceptual understanding of his own evolving consciousness and Spiritual awareness. As the story unfolds, the Author is continually challenged to redefine the views and beliefs he has been brought up with, and conditioned to accept.

However, by 'allowing' himself to be 'guided' and 'trusting' his own innate intuitional faculties, surprising and astonishing insights and abilities are revealed. These include the recognition of synchronistic events that have served to illuminate and illustrate a deeper understanding of what appears to be a major shift in Global Consciousness. Many individuals the Author has encountered and interacted with (especially through his work as a Spirit Guide Artist) are expressing a similar growing presence of a changing perception of themselves and the world they inhabit. Many are finding that this shift is particularly affecting their personal relationships. Perhaps there is a key here in that, as we explore, resolve and understand the relationship we are experiencing with our own selves, we could discover a whole new way of interacting and relating to that which appears to be external to ourselves - be it other beings or our environment.

The complexity of the times we live in and the acceleration of the development of technologies (intended to be for our benefit), coupled with the increase in worldwide communications systems, it is no wonder that some of us are experiencing an 'overload' in terms of the amount of diverse 'information' bombarding us daily. There are events occurring throughout the planet that are the direct results of decisions and choices that in many instances appeared to be based on genuine well intended beliefs. However, not all have necessarily produced a beneficial or benign outcome...or so it seems.

The Author however, has intuitively, or perhaps *chosen* instinctively at some deeper level of consciousness, to uphold the notion that there is an inherent quality of love and goodness at the core of every conscious living being and so has endeavoured to live his life accordingly. So whilst there may be a plethora of traumatic, dramatic and fear inducing doom and gloom stories that are the main themes on Television and in Newspapers, the Author chooses to view all the experiences facing humanity, regardless of whether they are considered good or bad, as being Teachers that are further intended to benefit us all.

Choosing to nurture an empowering way of being and developing the ability to respond as a co-creator of our perceived realities could perhaps be one of the most exciting and extraordinary challenges humanity has ever faced. Throughout history Art, Music, Poetry and a wealth of other art forms including Dance, have often served as an incredible source of inspiration and still do in many existing cultures. It could be conceived that we stand on the threshold of experiencing a whole new dynamic dimension of expression in our lives, as we consciously co-create new art forms to source our inspiration.

The Author extends an invitation to join him in the exploration and adventure of discovery and manifestation of some of these new art forms that could serve as inspirations for the new millennia, and further suggests that a starting point may be in the simple practice of the ART OF LIVING through the ART OF BEING.

***BECOME THE LIGHT OF YOUR OWN STAR!***

## Introduction by the Author

The amazing ability to adapt and accept new possibilities or concepts is matched only by my resistance to the same. Thus, I discovered that life is a seeming paradox, where both light and shadow inter-play their existence together in the same space. My experiences in life seem to be inextricably linked to what I hold as my belief at any given moment. Trying to hold onto set beliefs, no matter how altruistic, often seemed to be one of my greatest causes of anxiety and suffering.

Beliefs seem to be based on choices i.e., that which I choose to believe. There are of course beliefs that we inherit from our parents and environment which have a major impact on the belief we hold of ourselves.

Who could conceive of experiencing the persistent company of one specific individual throughout all of our entire conscious existence? Moment by moment, hour by hour, days, weeks, months, years…the same individual is consistently there with us watching and observing our every action, thought and deed! It would be quite understandable to comprehend that the consistent and unerring presence of this one individual could drive any normal person insane or at the very least bore us to distraction! Well, are we not our self that very one individual that consistently accompanies our self throughout our entire journey in life? Do we not hold a continual dialogue with ourselves discussing all the various experiences that life presents us with? It is curious that there has been a generally expressed view that people who talk to themselves are considered mad and yet the fact that some of us are actively engaged in a ceaseless never ending internal conversation with our self is considered normal! Sometimes this one 'self' can be very comforting, wise and empowering - oftentimes displaying remarkable talents, insights and understanding. Sometimes however, this very same individual can be a right pain in the 'butt', continually interfering, criticising and judging every single thought, word or action we undertake, and yes - on very many occasions this individual can be just plain tiresome, tedious and boring.

There is however, a quality of this constant companion and sometimes wayward child that is one-self that far supersedes all others and that is the facilitation and experience of a deep and all-encompassing sense of love and compassion - a Spiritual sense of unity and oneness with all creation - and what I choose to refer to as the 'Star' of our own being.

Join with me now and share in the journey and exploration of one such individual accompanied by their *one self* in the quest to manifest and become their own *Star-Being.*

*Enjoy!…*

### Chapter One: Climbing Trees

I cannot in all honesty recall much about what I thought about when I was born and apart from a very brief instant when I perceived some weird thing looking at me from beyond the car window (which I later found out was a cow), I do not recall much before the ages of about 5 to 7 years old. Climbing trees in the garden seemed to feature and absorb much of my conscious moments. Other consistent memories that spring to mind, includes being encouraged to draw by my Mum who always seemed to be singing opera (*Gilbert and Sullivan* and *My Fair Lady* were consistent favourites). I remember seeing *Watch With Mother* on TV and if I wasn't bouncing off the sofa and landing headfirst onto the fire hearth, I was falling headfirst out of trees! I still have memories of being carried bodily by my Mum and having my head thrust under the cold water tap. Heaven forbid my ever going bald as I must have a head that resembles the lunar surface!

I was born 2nd December 1949 in Bromley, Kent UK. My Dad was a Commercial Airline Pilot and in the early years worked mainly abroad. My Mum stayed at home bringing up myself and my two brothers - Martin (18 months older than I) and Graham (4 years younger).

I cannot recall what kind of thoughts used to occupy my mind during those many childhood hours spent up trees. However I do recall feeling completely contented and absorbed in those big friendly branches. Even when I started school, I couldn't wait to get home and play in the garden and of course the trees. Some of my other early memories were not quite so pleasant. This was that strange, eerie and scary world of childhood illness. I used to run very high fevers when I got ill and suffered hallucinations. One that frequently occurred was seeing what looked like a ball of cotton suspended in space continually winding itself round and round, and I had the sense that this process was eternal and never changed - the thought of which filled me with a sense of despair. Another was perceiving a room of seemingly normal appearance, that was lit by an overhead light bulb that hung bare and sparse in the absence of a lampshade. The disturbing element that concerned me was that of the dimness of the light and I experienced great distress at being unable to turn the brightness up (even to this day I dislike rooms lit with overhead light). Another strange fever induced childhood memory of this era was witnessing my Mum and visiting auntie frequently check in on me to see if I was all right - it seemed like they would do it in slow motion which absolutely terrified me! At one point I even saw them as Apes!

By the age of 7 to 8 years old a new preoccupation was starting to engage my conscious mind. As I relate this little snippet of my early history, I would like to state that I utterly and completely carry no grievance whatsoever towards my parents, for I know beyond a shadow of a doubt that there was no conceivable malice or harm ever intended in what would be generally considered harmless fun. At this impressionable and sensitive age, I was receiving the general instruction and compulsory indoctrination from school regarding the parameters and guidelines for conduct that is considered right or wrong, good or bad, or even good or evil! I had of course, had a sense of this already from my parents, which, I generally understood as "yes" was good and "no" was bad. Alternatively, a slap was the result of being bad, and treats or sweets were the result of being good (if only life were so simple)!

Generally in the years of my schooling, Religious education was compulsory and I was being told wonderful stories about God who is good and his wonderful son named Jesus who was kind and loving and performed wondrous miracles such as healing the sick. I can recall feeling an incredible sense of marvel at the stories that centered around this remarkable human being and felt so inspired by these stories, that I decided that I would like to be just like Jesus. I was however, also informed of another being during these early and impressionable years of my indoctrination. Oh yes, you guessed it, the old codger himself - 'Old Nick' or more frequently referred to as the Devil or Satan. Well, as you may imagine, my name also happens to be Nick and the harmless fun I related to earlier regarding my parents, was that of being frequently teased about growing horns and a tail like the Devil's - especially if I did not behave myself. I cannot recount the number of nights over a period of successive years, that I lay awake searching for signs of bumps on my head or any indication of a tail! The preoccupation I also referred to earlier that was starting to occupy my expanding consciousness on a fairly regular basis at this time, was that of the very serious contemplation of whether I was good or whether I was bad! Thus began at this oh so tender young age, my first real inner conflict.

On a lighter note (but no less puzzling to my young impressionable mind) regarding the unintended harmful comments that my parents made to me, I can frequently recall that, whenever something seemingly unusual happened, like perhaps when there was what may have been a knock at the door, or maybe an unexplained sound - whenever I questioned these, my Mum would say that it was "Jimmy Bung"! Who the heck is he?! To this day I do not know! The other common one was that whenever we were going out somewhere I would ask where we were going and the response would inevitably be "There and back to see how far it is"!

I have often pondered about the strange, curious stories that parents tell their children. Apart from those that are simply out of convenience, I often think that some of the curious tales are woven because, perhaps, the parents do not know the answers to some of the persistent questioning of their enquiring offspring. I know I drove my parents up the wall when I got older with my constant questioning of "Why?" to anything they told me. As very small children there is a tendency to think that parents know the answers to everything and it is not until they grow older that they realise that much of what their parents know and understand has been handed down from the generation before them. Of course there is a modification to some of the information, as each successive generation questions the validity of what has previously been upheld as an appropriate viewpoint. Then of course there are the general views or beliefs that are upheld by society at large, some of which may not be questioned at all. This raises the interesting question as to whether these larger general views or beliefs are how things really are, and are they really beneficial to the individual or are they just for convenience? For who is it, that decides the general views and beliefs of society? For that matter who is the 'authority' or the 'they' that are generally allured to as the creators of the laws or rules that humanity must adhere to?

To a large extent, Religions seem to have played a very significant role in the general widespread views that the public at large abide to. I was no exception to the seeming influence that the role of Religion played in my early childhood, most of which I gained from the schools I attended, for neither of my parents were particularly Religiously inclined. They did not however, discourage my keen interest in the subject.

The childhood memories I have of the early upbringing with my parents, seemed to be quite happy and as I mentioned previously most of my time was spent with my Mother due to my Father's occupation abroad. It was therefore down to my Mother to administer the general discipline and although at times my Mum could be quite strict, there was always an abundance of love and comfort. And it was always a jolly and exciting occasion when my Dad came home as he would invariably be laden with all sorts of goodies, and very often he would bring back some strange looking oddities that were representative of the local cultural artwork of the countries that he visited. I can recall one time when he brought home some African masks made of wood that I thought were really freaky - they had really long faces and earlobes to match! Then, one day on one of these occasional homecomings when I was about 9 years old and we had since moved to Crawley in Sussex, my Dad called all the family together and asked us all how we would feel about living in India for a year! You can imagine the excitement my two brothers and I felt at this extraordinary prospect and adventure placed before us. Going abroad to live in another country - talk about a reality shift!

## Chapter Two: Chapattis and Pecan Pie

It is amazing to comprehend how, in just one single year of one's life, one could have such an immense variety of diverse experiences. The year I spent in India was one such year and it was to have a profound effect on my developing perceptions of life.

Before we actually moved to India, we stayed for a month in Karachi, which is in Pakistan. My most immediate experience was that of the heat and lack of greenery. However, the excitement of being in a foreign land was much more overwhelming. We stayed in a hotel for the first few days, which in itself was a novelty. I was however in for a shock at mealtime when I was served this dark brown liquid, which my Dad (after considerable probing from myself) revealed to be turtle soup - yeeuck!

Funny is it not, how our immediate reaction to that which is unfamiliar to us is generally met with the above kind of response. Needless to say, I had great difficulty in the consumption of the aforementioned liquid brown soup and I need not go into my response to the turtle eggs that were next on the menu! Imagine how I further felt as a young lad when we went on a day trip to the coast and saw real live turtles gaily swimming in the sea.

Almost immediately after our arrival in Karachi, I was struck by the poverty that seemed to be prevalent amongst the general populace. No matter where we went, young children would surround us, begging for money. Everywhere we went - there were beggars and cripples lining the streets. I found it very distressing, for here was my first real first hand experience of human suffering. I was further startled at witnessing the local Pakistani men and women simply squat anywhere in the streets to do their 'business' and their only lavatory paper was that of a stone! Other surprises were of a lighter Nature, like seeing water buffalo leisurely strolling down the road, or the little lizards called geckos scurrying all over the place. Being woken at the crack of dawn by the bray of donkeys (a common form of transportation) was a bit startling as were the cockroaches that were a common feature around the house.

By comparison, India was seemingly less poverty stricken than Karachi, although there were still beggars to be seen and children would suddenly appear from nowhere begging for money whenever we were out and about. However, my first impressions of India on our arrival, was of how colourful the local folk were and the wonderful silken drapes the women wore, called saris. There was also these unusual passenger-carrying vehicles that were for hire called rickshaws that were either powered by bicycle or some form of motor scooter. I thought they were great fun and again, like everything else, the shops, the buses, and even the general transport lorries, were all gaily coloured.

The part of India we had moved to was called New Delhi and was fairly modern by comparison to other parts of India. There were modern shops and hotels as well as the more traditional market stalls and street traders who would relentlessly hassle you to buy their wares. I was fascinated by the merchandise that was being displayed on rows of carpet along the roadside. There was all manner of local arts and crafts, from elephants carved from ivory to exotic looking hubble-bubble pipes. Occasionally, there would be a snake charmer drawing large crowds of spectators. It was all utterly fascinating to behold. Colour seemed to play an important part in the lives of the Indian people. I can recall a particular festival that was celebrated once a year, where everybody starts the day off dressed in immaculate white outfits and then, armed with coloured paint loaded into a spray pump or just simply made up in buckets, one is then encouraged to spray or splash as many people as one likes so that by the end of the day the once immaculate white outfits are completely covered in multi-colours! It was glorious fun, tainted only for me by one little incident that I was not particularly impressed with. An Indian gentleman appeared as if from nowhere and thrust coloured paint powder into my mouth! This really quite distressed me, however, our neighbours who were local Indians informed me that this was considered lucky and I was to view the experience as a great honour!

The area we lived in was not particularly lush in greenery, although there was a small area of scrubland next to the house and thankfully it had some trees! When I was not climbing trees, I use to amuse myself with my two brothers making up amazing stories centred around some of our toy animals, for there was no TV to watch and we therefore had to create our own entertainment. Funnily enough, the absence of TV did not unduly perturb us, for there were plenty of other enjoyable stimuli to preoccupy us. One of which was regularly attending an outdoor swimming pool in one of the plush hotels about an hours drive away, located in Old Delhi. It was in this pool that I learnt and subsequently became an accomplished swimmer, both above and below water. We had a wonderful time on these occasions and regularly met and made many friends who were of a variety of different nationalities; German, Dutch, Australian and American. I can recall one particular occasion when we met some visiting American sailors who kept our whole family amused with stories of their exploits. As a special treat for us kids, they introduced us to what was evidently regarded by themselves (if their enthusiasm was anything to go by) as the highly desirable "Pecan Pie", served up in traditional U.S. marine standard ration packaging - devoid of any fancy labels - in plain tin cans. Mouth watering to be sure!

Since the subject of food has arisen, I remember the fascination I had at experiencing the making of chapattis, which were made from a special kind of flour mixed with water, and an oily butter type substance called ghee. I used to love watching with fascination, the way that these were prepared - it was a real art form. We had our own Cook as was common for most families - including the Indians to all seemed to have servants. Our Cook was a dab hand at making these chapattis. I spent many a pleasant hour watching and chatting away to him and learning about his culture.

Who could conceive that the simple subject of chapattis could serve to be a powerful catalyst in my understanding of growing awareness? For it is this very subject that brings to mind a rather shameful prank my brothers and I thought would be fun to play on a young man that used to regularly approach our house begging for food. Generally the servants would accommodate the young fellow and on this particular occasion, the prank we had in mind was to cut out a round piece of cardboard and send it out to him, pretending it to be a tasty chapatti. It is amazing how, in the briefest of moments one can experience two completely contrasting emotions, for in one instance I was laughing and giggling innocently at my brothers as they eagerly cut out the cardboard replicas of a chapatti, and then in the next split moment, I was filled with a tremendous sense of remorse and guilt at the prospect of the reaction of the poor young fellow on receiving a piece of cardboard for his daily meal! I was obviously experiencing the first sense of empathy and compassion that must have been stirring and at last being awoken in me since our arrival in this mysterious and enigmatic land.

I was starting to learn, from my own personal experiences, a sense of what *is* and what *is not* appropriate behaviour, which at this point in my life I interpreted as being 'right' and 'wrong'.

I made mention earlier of my growing preoccupation with this very issue and the perpetuation of this process was further advanced by the school which I attended whilst in India, which was run by the Anglican church. The repetition of the stories of the compassionate, loving and miraculou healer Jesus was furthering my conviction to follow in his footsteps.

We returned to England after a year spent in India. I was now 10 years old and whilst looking for somewhere more permanent to live, we resided for a month in a caravan. This was a novelty to my brothers and I, but I don't think it impressed my Mum too much. This little brief episode in my life was highlighted by the music we used to hear on the radio - *Apache* by *The Shadows* was a chart topper of the day. Eventually we moved to a house in Eastbourne, which was on the Sussex coast and features the well-known Beachy Head Lighthouse. Apart from the cold weather, I was excited to be back in the lush green land of England. There were plenty of woodlands and trees to indulge myself in. My parents bought me a bicycle and suddenly a whole new world was available to me and I took full advantage of this newfound freedom.

For some strange reason, I started to have strange dreams during this period of time where I was able to levitate my bike and would find myself flying high above an extraordinarily lush green landscape that filled me with an incredible feeling of oneness. I enjoyed going to school and it wasn't very long before I joined both the Boy Scouts and the Church Choir. This was a memorable time for me, which was further enhanced by the local Vicar who ran the church. He was, as I recall it, a very amusing and friendly character who smoked like a trooper. He sported a big bushy beard that seemed to enhance his friendliness. I can remember frequently being invited after the Scout sessions, round to the Vicarage where he would indulge my friends and I in teaching us card games amidst a haze of smoke (what a role model)!

It was at this point in my life that I discovered what I thought was to be my vocation... to become a Vicar!

Two and a half very pleasant years passed by and I was about 12 and a half years old when my Dad announced to the family that another opportunity abroad had been offered to him. This time the destination was to be Aden in Saudi Arabia! Yet another new adventure and experience was upon me to explore.

## Chapter Three: Music and the Desert Sun

The three years my family and I spent in Aden were for me a mixed bag of experiences. One that was not particularly pleasant was the early period of attendance at an all boys Catholic run school. I was continually taunted by the local Arabian schoolboys, due to being the only 'white' boy in the class. Here I was experiencing, first hand, being on the receiving end of racial discrimination. I also became very quickly aware that there was a high degree of sexual frustration prevalent amongst the Arab culture, probably due to the fact that their particular Religious faith forbade their women from exposing any part of their physical body, including their faces. The majority of Arab women wore plain black clothing that covered them from head to toe and they further had to wear a veil that covered their faces - no wonder they were frustrated! I had to bear a continual assault from the boys in my class as they tried to keep touching me during lessons. Because the Teacher of the class was a woman, I was too embarrassed to tell her. I also had other encounters with the local Arab boys that were equally unpleasant. These were numerous occasions when I was out and about, sometimes alone and other times with friends, when, without any provocation from ourselves, stones would be hurled at us by the Arab boys. Sometimes we would retaliate - resulting in a full-scale battle.

Of the more pleasant experiences, I really enjoyed the time spent at a swimming club we frequently visited. The club was positioned by a beach that was sectioned off by a large net fence to keep out the sharks! It was a great social life, especially during the holidays when some of the other Pilot's children that were at boarding school would come over. This period of time was the early music era of *The Beatles* and it was fantastic listening to "She loves you yeah, yeah, yeah" with all the chums on the beach (better than *Baywatch*)! It was just as well the social life was so good, for there was little else very appealing about the country for me - just sand, more sand, very hot weather and not many trees!

The area we lived in, was occupied predominantly by British Pilots and some of their families, and a short distance away was a British Army Base, so I made plenty of friends and there was always a party going on somewhere. I attended Church for a short period of time until I realised that I did not really like the atmosphere that I was increasingly sensing - that of oppressiveness. However, I persevered a short while longer due to the attendance of a very attractive young lady I fancied! Guilt eventually got the better of me though and I stopped going altogether.

I was now starting to find a new preoccupation that was attracting my attention... girls! To be more precise - girls and pop music - for I was increasingly spending a lot of time listening to the top twenty charts that were broadcast on the British Forces Overseas radio station. I started buying all the latest chart singles. *The Beatles*, *The Rolling Stones* and *The Hollies* to name but a few, and I spent many hours accompanying the records, drumming away on cardboard boxes with a couple of sticks.

My experiences with girls on the other hand were not quite so memorable, as I was extremely shy and self-conscious and though there were a number of young ladies I really liked, I was simply not confident enough to approach them. I did however, have a companion of a different kind - this was my pet dog, who I named Ted. I loved this dog dearly and we were inseparable, spending many happy adventures together. There was a rather strange and perplexing story attached to the circumstances that led to my parents allowing me to own a pet dog, for I had been continually pestering my parents regarding this matter ever since I first laid eyes on the batch of puppies our neighbours introduced us to, and I was consistently met with an emphatic "No". However, one particular night I suddenly woke up with a distinct thought, which was to go and see if my Mum was all right and whether she needed anything. I knocked on her door and was greeted with my Mum sobbing, sitting at the end of her bed. She immediately hugged me and explained that she was very depressed living here in Aden and had got so low that she had lost the will to live. Sitting at the end of her bed, she had written a prayer asking to be shown one good reason as to why she should carry on.

At that precise moment I knocked on her door enquiring as to her well being! My Mum was so overwhelmed that she gave me permission to choose one of the puppies. Here I was again, faced with another enigma to puzzle over and to add to my ever growing sense of "Something, I knew not yet what" stirring within my being.

The three years spent in Aden soon flew by and just prior to our return home, a major unrest started to break out between the British and the Arabs. My Dad had frequently commented on being shot at when flying over an area known as the Yemen. Fortunately, the rifles that were being used only had a very short range and were not very powerful, so no real harm was inflicted on my Dad and the other Pilots. I was glad we were leaving and I would certainly not miss the place, however, I was deeply saddened by the fact that we were not allowed to take Ted the dog with us, due to quarantine laws. We eventually found him a new home and bid him farewell. Once again we were winging our way back home to the lush green landscape of England. What was in store for me next I pondered!

## Chapter Four: Peace, Love and the Wild Man of Borneo

On our return to England we moved into a modern bungalow in Bognor Regis, Sussex. One of the other pilots and his family, whose son Mike had become a close friend of mine in Aden, also moved into the same area, so at least I had a chum to keep me company. I was excited to be back home and equally excited by the music that was bursting forth from the charts. My favourite radio station was *Radio Luxemburg*. It was also great being able to watch TV again. So much to catch up on! The news however was full of doom and gloom - this was the era of the 'Cuba Crisis' and atomic bombs. Some of the songs being played reflected the times, such as, "We're on the eve of destruction". Changes were afoot in the world and I was about to receive a few personal shock waves!

I was now 15 years old and sent to an all boys school (yet again) in Chichester. Almost immediately on hearing that I had just been living in Saudi Arabia, the boys at the school imposed not one, but two nicknames for me - one was "Lawrence" (as in Lawrence of Arabia) and the other was "Mamood"! Neither particularly enamoured me. I was now experiencing being an 'alien' in my own country! I became the object of fun to a particular gang of boys who would continually ridicule and harass me during break times. It became a regular occurrence to find myself being chased by this gang, and if they ever caught me (which was actually rare for I was a pretty nifty runner) I put up such a struggle that I invariably escaped. I am actually surprised at the way I took all of this in my stride and kept my good humour, to the extent that in the end, I had the gang of boys all laughing and eventually the tone of the assaults on me shifted to become that of a 'fun' challenge rather than a mocking harassment.

My other culture shock was that of a girl's school immediately adjacent to ours that shared half of the playing field. I was totally unprepared and unaccustomed to the ritual 'Kiss Chase' that was also common sport during break.

I did eventually settle in to my new school and made a few very good friends. At one point though, I remember becoming a little distressed to discover that a number of boys (and girls) were taking some form of drugs known as 'Purple Hearts'. I found it too baffling to comprehend and steered right away from it.

This period of time was in the early beginnings of the 'Mods' and

I can recall feeling quite envious of some of the older fourth year school boys turning up on Vesper motor scooters, dressed in trendy clothes and *Parker* jackets. Generally they would have the further accompaniment of a gorgeous Mod 'Dolly Bird' sitting astride the passenger seat. One Bob Dylan song certainly reflected that indeed the times were most certainly "a changing". We had only been back in England for about eight months and just before my sixteenth birthday (when my Dad had promised to buy me a second hand motor scooter) my Dad announced to the family that we were to go overseas again. The destination this time was to be Borneo in Malaysia!

So once again I was airborne, which by now was becoming almost second Nature. I celebrated my birthday on the airplane and our first stop over on route to Borneo was to be in Singapore on the mainland of Malaysia. It was a very exciting city and we stayed overnight in a plush hotel. I felt a bit like *James Bond* on one of his glamorous assignments! The next day my family and I went out exploring the shops and to buy me a birthday present. My Dad asked me what I would like to which I replied "A drum kit". My Dad's response to say the least was quite reticent. Not surprising really, as not only are drums quite expensive, we were already over laden with bags of luggage and could well do without the extra burden of lugging a drum kit along as well. So after a bit of persuasion I settled for a guitar instead, which I was quite happy about.

Borneo was very different to the previous countries we had lived in. It was mainly lush jungle and we lived in a town called Jessleton (now known as Kota Kinabalu) which was located quite near the coast. It was the epitome of a tropical paradise, with expansive sandy beaches,

palm trees and tropical islands. The Malaysian people were very friendly and I was intrigued by their culture. Imagine my delight on the first few days of our arrival, witnessing a 'Dragon Dance' procession accompanied by fire crackers, passing our front door - for we had arrived during the celebrations of their New Year. I was aware of a mystical enigmatic aura pervading this country and it's people. We soon settled in, but it was not long before I found myself adopting the role of peacemaker, as my two brothers started to increasingly be at each other's throats whenever our parents were out, and when I was not attending to their differences, I was caught in the crossfire of my Mum and Dad's disputes. Fortunately, these occurrences lessened as time went on. I was once again sent to a Priest run school. This one however was a mixed boys and girls school and it took me a while to settle in as I was starting to find it increasingly difficult, within the area of certain subjects, to understand the schools different curriculum. All the chopping and changing of schools over the years was taking its toll on my academic education. The only subjects I excelled in were English and Art, which came naturally to me.

My time at this particular school however, was to be short-lived. It had always been my inclination to be naturally friendly and I would always offer a smile towards any of the other students in the school be it male or female. On one particular day, I was called in to see the Headmaster (who was actually a Canon) and he immediately proceeded to accuse me of being a sex maniac! He had evidently, as had I, heard the stories coming from Britain and America regarding the new youth movement. This was the 'Swinging Sixties', the early beginnings of 'free love' and "Flower Power" and I got the full frontal assault of the views and opinions he held regarding the low moral values of the British youth, of which he seemed to have labelled me to be a representative of. He told me to cease smiling at the girls and further went on to warn me of not inflicting my undesirable and decadent influence on any of the other students! As you can imagine, I was flabbergasted to say the least! My response to this totally unwarranted onslaught was absolute fury. I could feel the raging heat well up inside me - I felt I could take on the world! However, I rang my Dad instead and when I told him what had occurred he was as furious as I was and in no time at all, he was down to the school and giving the offensive insulting Canon - a bit of his own medicine.

I begged my Dad to take me away from the school, which be did there and then without hesitation. I had experienced yet another example of the growing disenchantment I was feeling towards the oppressive attitudes and hypocrisy that seemed to prevail within some of the large established Religious organisations. I had barely even kissed a girl at this point in my life, let alone been a contender and purveyor of 'free love'! On the other hand, the Canon Headmaster although married, was carrying on an affair with his secretary!

I was also quite surprised to discover that the majority of the local Malaysians had been converted to Catholicism. I had an even greater surprise in store when I met a Malaysian girl, who was actually two years older than me and became my first real romance. As we got to know each other better, there was the natural (though scary for me) arousal of feelings. I had no experience whatsoever with courting young ladies, but I really wanted to kiss this girl. I was hoping that as she was older than me and had a boyfriend already (who she was supposed to be engaged to!), that she would instigate the move. Needless to say, she did not and I had to muster up all my confidence, which was practically non-existent and make the first move. What a disappointment I received when she refused! You can imagine my further dismay when she explained that she really wanted to, but that the particular brand of Catholicism she was indoctrinated by, forbade kissing before marriage! So I had to be content with holding hands and even that was considered risqué. Eventually however we did kiss, but it was not without an overwhelming shadow of guilt. Although on the brighter side, it may have made the whole thing that much more exciting. Unfortunately, guilt got the better of my girlfriend and she broke off our rather tenuous relationship. I was, as you can imagine, heart broken and was now experiencing a whole new and perplexing set of feelings and emotions to contend with. I moped around the house for weeks.

I had during this time settled into another school, however, my interest in the school curriculum was fast fading. I would sooner have been at home playing the guitar, for I had

taken to it like a duck to water and in no time at all had taught myself to play from a simple book of chords and was soon strumming all the tunes. There was a slight time warp in respect of the music that was generally aired on local radio, for the 'latest' sounds being played were at least ten years behind the UK and USA. The favourites were *Cliff Richards and The Shadows*. Every single local pop band knew the same repertoire. I tried to introduce *The Rolling Stones*, *The Beatles* and *The Kinks* to the locals but it was received rather dubiously. Although there was a large contingent of British, American and Australians to befriend, I had made several very good friends that were Malaysian and I joined a number of local bands. It was quite fun learning all *The Shadows* songs on the guitar, as it turned out.

As with the other countries I had lived in, the social life centred around the beach clubs and there was certainly no shortage of activities to indulge in. I took up sailing and water skiing and it was great fun taking off in either a sailboat or motorboat and exploring the nearby islands. There were plenty of parties and I looked forward to the summer holidays when all the boarding school students came over. I was quite envious of the trendy clothes that were becoming fashionable in England and which they all wore.

A year had now passed and suddenly my Dad announced that we were to move to Singapore, as there were greater career opportunities for him there. However, this turned out to be a very brief interlude and we were back in Borneo after just one month. I found it an interesting little period, particularly as they had TV in Singapore, which we avidly watched. The year was 1967 and most of the programmes were the latest produce from America. It was here that I first saw what was to become my favourite program - *Star Trek*. Another favourite was *Bewitched*. However, apart from the telly, there was not a great deal to do, and there was no beach club to visit or the associated facilities we had enjoyed so much in Borneo.

Once back in Borneo again though, we more or less carried on as before we left. I was becoming more disinterested in school and used to play truant with a new friend I had made - an African American young man named Danny. I can remember having very interesting debates with this new chum. We were almost like chalk and cheese, for there were many areas of seemingly conflicting viewpoints on a number of varying issues. One in particular was regarding girls and sex. Danny found it incredulous that I had never indulged in this particular arena and found me even more perplexing when I expounded the high moral values I upheld. His comment on my expressions of Spiritual views and values was "How come a cool regular guy like you maintains the kind of outlook generally associated with nerds and bookworm types in the States?" - which I suppose I should have regarded as a compliment. It seemed that any lad that had not been initiated into the fine art of "bonking" by the time they were fourteen, were generally placed in the "nerdy" category. I however, seemed to be an exception to that particular limited viewpoint.

We did however share the same enthusiasm for science fiction and fantasy. I can remember Danny excitedly coming over clutching the latest *Scientific America* - a journal on the latest scientific discoveries that his Dad subscribed to. I can remember being totally absorbed and fascinated by the 'Mobius Twist' theory. When we weren't engaged in fantastic or controversial conversations, we were off on his motorbike (generally whilst being truant) to indulge in a new pastime I had embraced - this being the game of pool which he had taught me to play - I got quite good at it.

The other common interest we both shared in, was a passion for was playing the guitar, and it was Danny who first taught me the basic 'blues' guitar scale that was becoming a regular feature in much of the new underground music emerging from the psychedelic 'Flower Power' movement of the sixties. I can remember the incredible excitement I felt at being able to play the lead guitar break in *All Along the Watchtower* by Jimi Hendrix.

My adeptness on the guitar was becoming a major force in my life. By the time I was eighteen I was writing my own songs. My younger brother Graham showed a natural aptitude for playing the organ which my Dad had bought for the family and we spent many happy

evenings entertaining the rest of the family with our regular performances. I had also around this time, formed a band with two Australian brothers and two Scottish brothers. We initially called ourselves *The Bird Watchers* but soon changed it to *Granville Spec*, which was a bit quirkier. We played regularly at the local sports club dances, performing cover versions of the latest hits in the charts like *Louie Louie*, *Groovy Kind of Love*, *The Kinks*' *You Really Got Me* and *Hold Tight* by Dave, Dee Dozy, Beaky, Mick and Titch! Very often I would sneak in a few of my own compositions - it was a fantastic period in my life - I felt like a Star!

By now I had grown my hair long (which would be considered short by today's standards) and had started to make my own clothes, which comprised of a kaftan and massive flares inset in my jeans. I had found a pair of moccasins in the local shops and my outfit was complete. I was now the only hippy in Borneo! Well, not quite, as I still hadn't experienced 'Free Love' and I most certainly had not participated in LSD acid trips - in fact I found the whole drug aspect of the hippy era very disturbing and this aspect was further highlighted when one day I received a letter posted from Morocco. The letter was covered in amusing drawings and psychedelic mushroom images and turned out to be from my best friend Mike in Bognor, England. Evidently he had hiked his way out to explore the delights of Marrakech and Morocco and had written the letter 'smashed' out of his head on some psychotropic substance, crashed out on some root top under the stars. I was extremely disturbed and concerned about the well being of my good friend.

Regarding the other topic of 'Free Love' that was fast becoming the other major focus of the growing youth movement - I was completely baffled. I could however, identify with the concepts of "Peace and Love" and this alone was reason enough for me to embrace the growing generation of 'Beautiful People' and 'Flower Children'.

I was fast reaching the age of eighteen and by now I had attracted a number of very lovely girlfriends, however I could not bring myself to ever make any sexual advances towards them. One reason for this was because a lot of my close personal friends were female and I would be increasingly distressed on hearing some of my male friends make reference to some of these dear friends as mere sex objects. So, I would never allow myself to stoop so low and take advantage of any of my girlfriends. The other reason was a bit more nebulous, for somewhere I had picked up the strange notion that women didn't like sex! As a consequence of this, you can imagine my confusion when the relationships with my girlfriends abruptly ended and they would then go on to date some of the 'lusty lads' and end up having sex with them!!!...Did I not mention earlier on how life seemed to be a continual paradox?!

Prior to our last year spent in Borneo, I was now going on nineteen years old and I had started a correspondence course to continue my education, which I worked on from home. This required a tremendous amount of self-discipline on my part, as it was all too easy to get distracted. My elder brother Martin had been allowed to go back to England and continue his education there. I had wanted to do the same but try as I might my parents would emphatically disallow it. Their argument such as it was, was on the assumption that I would, as they put it, "Shack up with some dolly bird". That sounded great to me, but it was not to be. I was really missing England and all the exciting new music and happenings that I was hearing about.

I had experienced a few little tasters of these, during the short little bouts of 'leave' that we took as a family. This would generally only be for a couple of months back home in the UK, but it was enough to wet my appetite. We were due to embark on the last of these brief respites before finally coming home for good in the following year, when my Dad started to continually quiz me on what career I was going to pursue. Well I hadn't a clue! My Dad's patience with me was wearing a little thin, and he tried to make suggestions. Some of these included Art College - as I was always drawing and painting anyway, and Drama

School - as I had shown a natural acting ability when I had been roped into some theatre productions performed by the local Amateur Dramatic Society that my Mum had got involved in - which also included some set designing and painting - all of which I thoroughly enjoyed. One other suggestion that was made was that of becoming a Computer Programmer, as computers were starting to feature prominently in the world at large. All of these however, required at least five GCE O levels. I decided that Drama School might be favourite and wrote to several, but I never received a reply.

Whilst back in England on our final leave, my Dad took me to the nearest Art College which was located in Worthing, Sussex. I had a promising interview and subject to attaining the mandatory GCE qualifications, they approved my application. I subsequently spent the majority of our leave with my nose to the grindstone. I was quite proud of my earnest application to the task at hand and regularly set the clock for 6am and got stuck in before the rest of the family arose. I think that I was even more surprised at my new found determination and freshly acquired self-discipline than my parents were, particularly as during this brief period back home and whilst attending a party, I had met a new young lady who became my new girlfriend and with whom I obviously wanted to spend as much time with as I could. Yet I devised a schedule to divide my time in such a way as to accommodate both, and strictly adhered to it.

My good mate Mike also turned up during this leave and it was a great reunion - we had much to catch up on. His arrival to our bungalow in Bognor was quite a spectacle, as he drove up on a bright silver Vesper motor scooter, decked out with flags, stickers and fluffy bits. He too had grown his hair long and was sporting a trendy corduroy jacket and suede desert boots, painted black with large white polka dots! Mike had also applied to the same Art College that I had, which only served to further my determination to achieve the necessary qualifications.

It was not long before Mike and I were locked into our usual deep and meaningful discussions, which had become an increasingly regular feature of our long-standing friendship. Although, on the face of it we appeared to hold seemingly opposite views, there was never a shortage of subject matter for us to explore and debate for hours on end. Most of these discussions would generally take place during our frequent visitations to the local seashore, for we both loved being out in Nature. I naturally quizzed him on his frequent use of psychedelic substances, which I still had a hard time trying to grasp and understand the necessity of indulging in. Mind you, I also found it equally baffling as to the need for the excessive quantities of alcohol that most folk indulged in, particularly when I had witnessed many occasions where the presence of this highly volatile substance had been the instigator of many an ugly scene, when the general gaiety and frivolity it seemed to induce, could be rudely interrupted by the smallest of comments or unintended gestures, resulting in the manifestation of the very worst in human behaviour. Mike however, quite happily indulged excessively in both substances with no seemingly adverse effects. His preference however, was towards the 'psychedelics'.

These two particular topics that I have mentioned were to cause me a great deal of bewilderment over the ensuing years, as my enjoyment and perceptions of life as I had been living it, had been sufficient unto itself and I simply could not understand why there was any necessity to ingest any external substances to experience a 'high', when to me, life itself was a high. What I did not realise at the time (and it would be many years on before I started to grasp it's significance) was that I was somehow probably intuitively or perhaps even instinctively cultivating a natural inherent sense of Spirituality that permeated and sustained my being and thus served as an inner stimulus and intoxicant, rather than the need for any that were external. During these early years, I had not yet developed any conscious conceptions of guidance emanating from this Spiritual source, other than that of an ever increasing sense of 'knowing' that lingered in some deep recess of my inner being. As I am writing this distant memory of the past, it has just occurred to me that it would probably be more correct to use the term 'knowing what is not', which could still arguably be considered a 'knowing'.

Throughout the many varied, sometimes colourful and delightful, and sometimes painful experiences I have participated in during my life, I have long perceived the early years of my life to be over laden with an elusive quality of knowing something but not knowing what it was I knew! No wonder I have spent a large portion of my life in a state of confusion! All the experiences I have had, regardless of the form they have taken - be it considered good or bad - have all been and served as powerful catalysts in assisting me in the redefining and refinement of my conscious understanding of my life.

With reference to my earlier comment on the 'knowing' and 'knowing what is not', my particular focus in life has been trying to grasp an understanding of what it was that I sensed I knew. Oblivious was I to the invaluable and profound gift I had been blessed with of knowing 'what is not' (talk about answers being right under one's nose)! To clarify these comments, I must refer back to the decision I had sincerely and earnestly expressed way back in my early childhood, which had been to aspire to the example that the individual known as Jesus (in the Christian Religion) had displayed and was further quoted as saying "All these things I do, you can do and more", which had inspired me to embrace the same ideals and principles I understood him to have expressed. Some of these included; extending love to all, developing tolerance and compassion, doing unto others as one would do unto one self, and the demonstrations of the astounding ability to facilitate healings, to name but a few. With respect to the 'miracles' of these - I was yet to conceive.

So far in my personal life I had to the best of my ability endeavoured to live and become an exemplification of all these ideals, of which I understood to be the framework for that which is termed 'Spiritual' or 'Spirituality'. Further more, the impression that I had conceived of as being the source of all these Divine principles - the entity generally referred to as God - must surely be the ultimate personification and expression of these very same principles. With this in mind, imagine my bewilderment when I began to discover that a very different God was being depicted and represented by many different established Religious belief structures and organisations that I encountered on my travels.

In the many diverse and colourful cultures of the countries I had visited up to now, I had observed that they too had their own equally revered Spiritual figure heads and deities that had displayed much of the same Divine attributes and abilities that Jesus had. As with Christianity these were represented by large Religious organisations, whose responsibility it was to maintain and uphold the dictates of the Spiritual and moral codes of conduct of their established Spiritual and Religious belief systems that were indoctrinated into their followers.

The God that was depicted by many of these doctrines was a wrathful God invoking fear and terror into the hearts and minds of the devoted men and women who were it's subjects. "Hell fire and damnation" awaited those that dared traverse and stray from the rigid rules and laws that were the mandates of these Religious and pious orders. If that wasn't bad enough they were doomed even before they started, being as they were supposedly "Born in sin" from the onset!

To be fair, there was at least an indication of salvation at the end of it all in the afterlife! That is of course providing they met with the necessary criteria in this life i.e., to follow unswervingly the decrees and mandates of their particular creed without question, sacrifice their free will and their life if need be (as well as a substantial chunk of their earnings). All in the name of the beneficent being they refer to as their God! "Where is the God of Love?" I asked myself? And in the context of what I was learning to understand and cultivate as my perceptions of true Spirituality was fast getting to know 'what is not'!

I was now 19 years old and in my final year in Borneo and I had much to ponder over. I was concerned for my friend Mike in England and his psychedelic exploits and I naturally missed my girlfriend. However, I had other more immediate concerns to contend with, as I had still more work to complete for my forthcoming exams.

In a twinkling of an eye they were upon me. Out of five subjects I took, I only passed three; Art, English Literature and English Language. The two I failed was Maths and Trigonometry which I had actually mastered, however, when I sat the exam I discovered that the correspondence course I had studied was a year out of date. I was naturally disappointed and all hopes of attending Art College seemed to be out of the window.

As a light relief some new friends popped briefly into my life - a young Dutch man named Hass, and Karen who was a gifted Artist. Through my introduction they became a couple and I spent many a pleasant hour or three in their company, engaged in fascinating conversations. The only occasions that my enthusiasm waned during these pleasant interludes was when the subject of politics arose. Mostly because of the highly emotive arousal of hostility that the subject seemed to induce in the normally most pleasant of folk. However, of the more pleasurable topics we explored, Karen introduced me to the delightful and inspiring works of a number of Artists from the 1920's who were exponents of *Art Nouveau* that derived it's themes and inspiration from Nature, particularly flowers - all colourful flowing images that were becoming increasingly evident in the Hippy 'Flower Power' artwork of the current times. Karen's work was much along these lines and she had painted a wonderful flowing mural on her wall. However, in spite of the exciting stimulus around me I slumped into a short period of dejection, mostly due to the increasing pressure to choose a career.

I had long since relinquished the idea of pursuing a Religious occupation due to the amount of hypocrisy I had witnessed in established Religions. I had passed the aptitude test for Computer Programming and had been accepted (regardless of the lack of qualifications). However, I could not raise the necessary enthusiasm to pursue it (I have often pondered where I would be now, had I chosen this course).

My despondency was further perpetuated when the two Australian *Granville Spec* band brothers invited me to emigrate to Australia and form a professional band over there with them. This was an exciting prospect, however as fortune would have it anyone wishing to emigrate below the age of twenty-one needed their parent's permission to go and as you have probably guessed, I was once again met with an emphatic "No" from my parents. To add salt to my already smarting wound, my elder brother Martin was funded and sent off to Colorado in the USA to train in his chosen career, which was to follow in my Dad's footsteps and become a Pilot.

So here I was left in a quandary. On top of this, news was coming in thick and fast of more impending worldwide disasters including; war, threats of atomic bombs, riots, and unwarranted police brutality being inflicted on participants of the 'Peace Movement' during their regular sit-ins. One poignant and poetic gesture that lingered long in my memory was that of a young group of 'Flower Children' placing flowers in the gun barrels of a military troop out on parade. This heartened and lightened my Spirits. So too did the music, which was increasingly expressing the ideals of love, peace and unity. This was also the era of transcendental meditation that many famous names were participating in - *The Beatles, Donovan, Moody Blues, The Beach Boys* and even Frank Sinatra come to mind, plus a host of celebrities in the acting profession. 'Love-ins' were the speciality of the day.

Elsewhere an ex-University Professor, Timothy Leary, was delivering with evangelistic fervour his message of "Turn on, tune in and drop out". The song *What's It All About Alfie* was certainly a poignant sentiment of the times.

Time flew by and it was only a mere few days before our departure from Borneo that an announcement was made on the radio - America was to send a man to the Moon! How curious and synchronistic that as a new chapter was to unfold in the world at large, so too was it to unfold in my personal life.

## Chapter Five: Here Comes the Sun

"Oh to be in England lad, all Summery joy!" - these words from Stanley Olwin, perfectly express how I felt to be back home.

We arrived back in England at the tail end of summer and there was a vibrant feeling of excitement and expectation in the air. Within a matter of weeks I had started my very first job, which was Apple Picking, and I loved it! I still have the fondest memories of this brief moment in time - how could I not, for here I was being paid to climb trees! What could be more delightful than being out in the sunshine, the sweet smell of the fruit of the tree pervading the airwaves, intermingling with the sound waves jangling brightly from my portable radio. *Here Comes the Sun* by *The Beatles* was a regular favourite along with a whole colourful array of weird and wonderful songs from equally weird and wonderful bands like *Tyrannosaurus Rex*, Jethro Tull, *King Crimson* and *Pink Floyd* to name but a few. This short little magical interlude in my life was to sow the seeds of a profound realisation that was to gently unfold and reveal itself in the ensuing years, as to being a major influence in the shaping of my ever-increasing sense of Spiritual awareness. For my closest feelings of oneness with the source of all things generally thought of as God, is when I am out in Nature, or when I am either listening to or creating inspiring music. So too was Art to become a major force in my life and shortly after the apple picking season was over, I made a determined decision to get into Art College. I wanted to show my parents that I could achieve things on my own, so without telling them I armed myself with bundles of sketches and paintings and marched confidently into the college head office, and low and behold I managed to talk my way in.

For the first time in the many varied experiences I have had of educational establishments, I felt at home. Or at least so I thought at first. The fact that my good friend Mike was also in attendance naturally furthered its appeal and so too did the fact that we could wear whatever we liked, in fact the wackier the better! It was great attending a class full of wildly individual characters with equally wild outfits. The course that I was embarking on was a one year Art Foundation course covering a variety of subjects, one of which could then be specialised in over a further three years. On my first day I was in for a bit of a shock, for I had been instructed on the various classes I was to attend during the day and one of these was Photography, which I was really looking forward to. However, on arrival at the class I was told there had been a mix up and I would not be covering this topic until my last term. Instead, I was to attend Pottery class! As a result of the mix up I was late turning up to the class. What I was met with was astonishing to say the least. For on entering the room full of students I was to witness a most disturbing display of bullying and intimidation, being demonstrated by the Teacher, as he totally demoralised and embarrassed a young female student he had pulled up in front of the class and whom he subsequently reduced to tears. Immediately after this he launched into an abusive attack on me for being late! I could feel my 'hackles' rising (which was a frequent occurrence whenever I witnessed a perceived injustice) and I very curtly explained my situation which somewhat diffused his aggressive stance.

I was in for another shock as I seated myself, when he called in the homework he had set the class the week before. The subject he had set for them to work on was to write a summary of... wait for it...*What do I think of myself as a student?* "What was this all about" I thought - as if this wasn't bad enough that he had hurled into a verbal attack on all of the students, expressing his evidently very low opinion of them!

What a start to my first day at college! The other tutors however, were far more pleasant and I soon settled in. I got on reasonably well with the course for the first few months, although I found some of the projects we were set a bit puzzling at times. Half the time I didn't even understand what we were supposed to be doing and my enthusiasm soon started to wane. The social life on the other hand was great and I made many friends. During the weekends we would frequently attend open-air music festivals, which were really exciting and featured a number of bands that were to become a great inspiration to me, one of these was a band called *Yes*. One of the other highlights of this first year in college was the formation of my own band, which was great fun, especially when performing for several of the college dances.

It was during one of these particular social events, that I was to meet a young female fourth year student, who was to eventually become my wife for the next ten years - her name was Ingrid.

As the year rolled on I was finding myself becoming increasingly disenchanted with the college's view of Art, which leaned heavily towards intellectualism. So about a month before the final end of the term - I decided to leave. Needless to say this decision did not go down particularly well with my parents and it wasn't long before my Dad started lecturing me again on the necessity of academic qualifications. I can still remember vividly on one of these frequent occasions when a rather strange sensation descended over my being and in that instant I found myself calmly and confidently walking up to my Dad and gently telling him that the career that was to become my own, would not need academic qualifications. As I spoke this out I had this extraordinary sense of knowing this was the absolute truth! Even though I had no idea at the time of what this career was to be. What was even more surprising was my Dad's response, which would have normally been argumentative. On this occasion though, he gently nodded in agreement and said that I was probably right! I spent the next couple of weeks visiting chums at the college and interspersing this with seeing my girlfriend Ingrid. Then, on one particular day, I decided I was going to get myself a job.

I can remember it being a warm sunny day in May and after purchasing a local newspaper, I went and sat on the beach. I was disappointed to find however, that there was absolutely nothing in the *Jobs Available* slot that I qualified for. I searched everywhere for jobs available in Art, but alas to no avail. Then an innovative thought struck me... I should go down to the local art shop and ask in there - it was obvious. The interesting facet of this little episode is that I had absolutely no experience in the realms of job hunting and subsequently I had no preconceived ideas as to how difficult some folk find it, particularly during times of heavy unemployment. I was however, oblivious to any of this, such was my naivety at the time and I confidently strolled into the art shop and declared myself to the assistant. "I am an artist" I said, "and I was wondering if you have any jobs available please?". The assistant who was a kind hearted elderly lady apologetically responded, explaining to me the difficulties artists generally face in respect to obtaining work. Barely had her words left her lips when a tall bearded Scottish gentleman introduced himself as Bob and said he was an Artist himself. He further went on to say that he ran a Portrait Studio at *Butlins Holiday Camp* and was looking for another Artist to work with him!

I received two gifts that day - one was obviously the job, but the other I was not to recognise for many a year. Its simple profundity was to have a major impact on my thinking…that of simply trusting and believing anything is possible!

And so began a completely new dimension in my life and I took to it as a duck to water. I started initially as his General Assistant and in the interim he taught me to draw portraits using pastels (a chalky type of crayon). My first attempts were a bit messy to say the least and I felt a bit worried that I might not get the hang of it. Then one evening I came into work to see a very distraught looking Bob, who anxiously explained to me that one of the other Artists that generally worked along side him, had let him down. He further went on to explain that they had both been fully booked with appointments for the entire evening. Talk about being chucked in the deep end! Yes, you guessed it, I stepped in and to say it was unnerving would be an understatement. The studio was situated in the corner of one of the main ballrooms and was consistently busy with holidaymakers the whole day through. Consequently, we had a constant stream of onlookers who surrounded us on practically all sides, not to mention those who overlooked us from the balconies and stairs above us! Furthermore, I could hear every word that was being spoken by the onlookers. Imagine how I felt on this first night when I could hear comments relating to how good they thought Bob's work was and would then make contrary remarks towards mine. It was one of those times when I wished the ground would swallow me up and I would silently request "Beam me up Scotty!".

Fortunately within a short space of time I had improved considerably, in fact so much so that eventually some people were expressing a preference to my work, which boosted my flagging confidence no end. Thus began a most extraordinary summer… and there was more to come!

## Chapter Six: And So It Begins

This was the summer of 1970 and I was 20 going on 21 years old. I spent the entire summer season drawing portraits at *Butlins*. I was paid 50p per portrait out of a total sum of £3.50 paid for by the client (£1.50 went on the frame). So where did the other £2.00 go I asked myself?! Well, 50p went to Bob as Manager and the remaining £1.50 went to *Butlins* in commission. I was only allowed 20 minutes per portrait and we averaged £20.00 per day, which is 100 clients a week - talk about intense! This earned me £50.00 per week, which was a reasonable income back in those days. It did not take me long however to realise that there might be an even more advantageous way of working things, but that was yet to come. In the meantime, I thoroughly enjoyed that summer as I had so much to look forward to. I regularly saw Ingrid and our relationship was steadily growing. Other times I spent with my good mate Mike. By now I had lessened the intensity of my self-righteous attitude towards him and drugs. Most of the college students had been experimenting with them, mainly LSD and Marijuana and I had engaged in many deep discussions with some of these students on the topic of drugs versus Spirituality. One student even lent me a book he thought I would enjoy; a written account of an individual named Carlos Castaneda and his experiences with a South American Yaqui Medicine Man who called himself Don Juan. Unfortunately, or fortunately, depending on one's view, all this book succeeded in doing at the time was to further my indignation and I can remember throwing it down in disgust after a couple of chapters believing it to be all about taking drugs. You can imagine therefore, the amount of serious contemplation, deliberation and reservation I had to wrestle with to ever consider taking them myself.

I did however try a sample of Marijuana which just gave me the giggles and left me wondering what all the fuss was about. LSD on the other hand was another matter. Was there any real significant value or benefit to be obtained or derived from the experience? Judging from the many horror stories circulating about from it's use i.e., people thinking they can fly and jumping from windows or other's so fascinated by the colours emanating from the Sun that they ended up going blind, left a lot to be desired. Oddly enough though the individuals that I personally met who had tried it gave a different story. Most expressed a profound sense of Spiritual oneness with all things, perceiving a connection with all of creation, which made me think "Hey! Wait a minute, this is my domain!". It was further explained to me that the experience one has from these commonly referred to 'trips' were the result of chemicals being released that are naturally inherent in the body and all the LSD does is to serve as a trigger to release it. "Hmm!" I thought...

And so it was one sunny Saturday morning, I set off with my friend Mike and headed for the park and lake nestled behind Arundel Castle, located in the hills and dales of the Sussex Downs. This was to be the chosen safe haven for my very first venture into the unknown and seemingly potentially dangerous territory. I had finally relented and on Mike's recommendation, we were going to share just one third of an 'acid tab' as they were commonly known. They generally took the form of a simple miniscule square or dot of blotting paper that had been soaked in LSD. These had a multitude of weird and wonderful names like *Purple Haze* and *Strawberry Fields* (they'd make good titles for some music tracks... wait a minute...what's this? *Lucy in the Sky with Diamonds*?!!!).

Mike bad been absolutely amazing in preparing me for what I was about to experience and my estimation of him rose considerably. He was to be my guide on this inexplicable journey into the unknown regions of perceptual consciousness, and I shall never forget his wise and comforting counsel.

We digested the tiny dot of blotting paper on the train journey to the park, as Mike explained it took a while to take effect. We disembarked at Arundel station and ventured into the park. It was a glorious day and I was filled with a mixture of anticipation and trepidation. Mikes easy going and amusing manner soon dispelled any further anxiety. The park was more or less empty, which suited me, although the place is so vast that even when its busy there's plenty of space and privacy, which is one of the reasons we chose it. I didn't notice anything out of the ordinary at first, but as I was looking down to the sun reflecting off the lake, this most  extraordinary flash of colour shot off in all directions. "Is that normal?" I thought. This query was to become my most commonly expressed sentiment throughout the entirety of this, my most unusual day out! Mike was off in the distance somewhere and didn't hear my exultations, presumably lost in some fascinations of his own. I made my way further up the hill and found a spot with an enchanting view of the lake below me, cushioned by the surrounding green and undulating hills. It was at this moment, that it occurred to me that the sensations that were now increasing in intensity were totally familiar to me, like some long forgotten tune or dream that suddenly emerges into conscious memory. Then something totally unprecedented happened as I switched on the portable radio I had bought with me. This is the best way that I can describe it; the music from the radio shot out in all directions simultaneously, bounced off the lake, then rang around the surrounding hills and back up into my eardrums, exploding in my head with the most incredible sounds - weird 'flanging' and 'phasing' with harmonic tones which I never even knew existed - or did I - for here again was that strange sense of familiarity.

I excitedly recounted my experience to Mike, who gave me a knowing look and burst into laughter, which likewise did the same dance as the music. His laughter was everywhere. I would have loved to have been watching this event from the perspective of a normal passing observer. For at that moment in time (or it seemed more like *no time*) I lost all perception of either the length or brevity of our transfixed joviality - not that it mattered, for the moment was enough unto itself, whether it be for an eternity or a billionth of a second - it was ever present. The moment however was abruptly halted as I observed in the distance across the lake, a young man dressed as a 'skin head' or 'bovver boy' as they are also known and they DO NOT LIKE LONG HAIRED HIPPY TYPES!..."Uh oh" I thought! "We have long hair"! "Run Mike Run!"...PARANOIA! PARANOIA..."He knows we're tripping - Run!!!".

Gasping for breath we reached the top of the hill, Mike calming me down on the way. "I didn't like that much at all!" I thought. However after a brief respite, I eventually managed to calm down. The next thing I knew, my attention was being drawn towards the bark of the tree we had been sitting at. My first impression was of how incredibly smooth it seemed. When I looked closer however, I now perceived it as an astonishing intricacy of unbelievable patterns that defy description and then when I looked closer again, the patterns likewise changed. Mike laughed heartily at the apparition of my total absorption and the accompanying expletives of "Corr", "Amazing" and "Wow!"

We wandered about the hilltops enjoying the moments, when we suddenly discovered we had wandered into a field of sheep. This completely startled me and for the life of me in that moment I could not remember whether sheep attacked people! To add to the weirdness of this encounter, they all had black faces and were all staring at me! Talk about being spooked. We quickly made our exit and then Mike suddenly had this great idea, "Lets go into town!" he said. "Whoa!" I said, that seemed far too hectic and further more they'd be loads of people! I don't know how he managed to persuade me, but before I knew it we were heading for town.

On our exit from the park, we encountered two elderly ladies, "Oh no! Look Mike!...Their faces are like plasticine!" I gasped and that wasn't to be my only moment of consternation during our walk about town. Suffice to say I did not enjoy it very much, particularly the brief pause we made outside a jewellery shop caught by the sparkle and glitter of it's displayed wares and in the midst of expressing our delight in the current vernacular of the times like "Wow! Too much man!", I caught sight of a Policeman on the other side of the road. Well I thought the skinhead encounter was scary, but this was something else! I honestly thought he knew we were on LSD and was going to arrest us! I had never experienced such a profound sense of paranoia and feeling of exposure as I felt in that instant. However, he didn't really take much notice of us and went on his way. That was it for me and I insisted we go back to the safety of the park, which we did.

By the time we got back home, the effects of the experience had considerably lessened, although there was still a semblance of weirdness lurking around, so we decided to go to thebeach which was only a short distance away. The sun was just setting as we arrived and it was a most spectacular sight to behold. The colours and the feelings that I felt emanating from them held me in an ecstatic rapture. I felt that now familiar sense of oneness permeate my being and I thought "What a glorious, close to extraordinary day"!

So, what were my thoughts on 'the psychedelic experience'? I could not answer this question immediately for I had much to digest and assimilate. The first thoughts I had were of how grateful I was to Mike for his guidance throughout and of how potentially hazardous and foolish it would be to partake of this substance indiscriminately.

I was to try this experience again on just one more occasion at this period in my life, and it would be another ten years before I ever dared venture into the strange and enigmatic world of chemically induced altered states of consciousness again.

On this second occasion, I had decided to increase the dosage to one half of a tab. A friend of Mike's provided me with the 'trip' and I was to meet Mike in a local park. After almost two hours of waiting past our prearranged time, I made an impulsive decision.

I took the whole tab! I can only describe it as being one of my most terrifying experiences. I lost all sense of time and I thought that it would never end. The panic I felt was almost indescribable and if it had not been for a girl, a friend of Mike's whom I had only met briefly once before, turning up, I do not know what I would have done! I begged her to stay with me until I had more control of my senses, which she kindly did.

What a peculiar and bizarre afternoon that turned out to be, me on the one hand groaning about wishing it would hurry up and end, whilst my kind companion on the other, continually kept on about wishing she had taken some herself!

Before I conclude this little episode, there was one more brief encounter that I found both puzzling and intriguing. After eventually finding the effect wearing off enough to make my way home, I had to walk through the town, which from my previous experience, I was not looking forward to. However, I managed to summon up the courage and endeavoured to act as normal as I could and made my way into town. As I feared, it was a disquieting experience, for there was a disturbing sense of alienation and disconnection. Then I saw an individual walking towards me with a flowing rhythm to his walk and there seemed to be a radiance shining forth from his being. As he passed, he gave me a warm friendly and knowing smile and in that instant I knew that he was also tripping!

What occurred next was even more inexplicable, for it almost seemed we had a telepathic rapport and in that moment he must have picked up the distress I was feeling, for he was suddenly consoling me and recommended that I stop off at some friends of his until I felt more settled. His final parting words, after giving me the necessary directions were "Don't worry, they will look after you", and sure enough, they did! I was greeted like a long lost friend as they ushered me into the lounge, which was inhabited by several more warm and friendly young people. They settled me in and in no time at all, I was as captivated as my hosts appeared to be by the waves of sound exploding and cascading out of the music system that was in evidence on my arrival. How poignant, that the track I was listening to (in a way that I had never before heard), was *Led Zeppelin's I Gotta Whole Lotta Love*!

The final conclusions, I drew from my assessment of this brief encounter with LSD could be summed up in the three following observations:-

1) Some of the experience scared the living daylights out of me and I would be very wary of trying it out again, if at all!

2) What I saw, sensed, heard, touched, felt and smelt, was as real to me as any other experience. The difference was in my perception. Things that I would normally either take for granted or pay little heed to, were fascinating to me and all had a potent and inexplicable link to the overall 'whole' that I felt as a feeling of oneness.

3) The fact that I perceived the experience as a reality and that it further affected and indeed even enhanced the awareness of my normal five physical senses, and even included a sixth sense if one includes the telepathic rapport that occurred on a number of occasions, implies to me that these abilities must be naturally inherent in our physical bodies and there must therefore be a natural means to access them.

I was not to wait long before the first piece of this puzzle was to fall into place and was to have an amazing impact and influence on the incredible journey of adventure and discovery that was to unfold in my life.

## Chapter Seven: The First Seeds are Sown

The summer of that first year of the 1970's was fast coming to a close, when my Mum summoned me and requested my company as moral support to an invitation that had been extended to her from one of her friends. This was to attend an evening demonstration at the local Spiritualist Church! My mind was to immediately fill with images of people sitting around a table all holding hands in a darkened room and a Medium at the head of the table, uttering in a theatrical manner "Is there anybody there?". I was however to be pleasantly surprised, for instead we were greeted by a wonderful warm, friendly and caring group of people who welcomed us with a genuine sincerity that I found quite refreshing. There was no darkened room, nor any of the theatrics that are often the view generally portrayed of Mediums and Spiritualists by the media of the day. Instead we were led to a room set out very much like a conventional church service, including an altar featuring a cross, surrounded by a colourful display of freshly cut flowers.

My first reaction was to recoil at the seemingly Religious overtones present in the decor of the room. However, I was soon to relax on discovering the absence of any conventional ordained Priests in attendance. It was further explained to me that Spiritualism is not considered a Religion, it is more a set of principles and understandings that could enhance the views and outlooks of a person's life regardless of their chosen Religious upbringing. Some of these principles included; the continuation of life after death and taking the form of a consciousness - generally referred to as the 'soul' or 'Spirit', the ability to communicate with those who have departed the physical realm, the ability to facilitate healing, the existence of the angelic realms, and the acknowledgement of the law of cause and effect i.e., "What one hands out, returns to them" - more often known as the law of Karma. I did not have any objection to these principles, in fact some of them were very similar to my own ideals.

The evening continued with an introduction to a guest Medium who, after a short opening speech followed by some hymns and prayers, proceeded to randomly select individuals in the audience and deliver them a message from loved one's in the Spirit World. I was fascinated by the response of the recipients of these messages, for they all confirmed the validity of the information given, particularly as most of it was related to personal things that only they would have known. What occurred next took me completely by surprise as the Medium directed his attention towards me! I was sitting (intentionally) right in the back row seats and I was starting to get concerned about the time and wondering how much longer the service was going to continue, as I had a date I was eager to keep with my girlfriend Ingrid. The Medium's opening words to me were "Haven't you got time to live lad"?. I immediately started to inwardly panic and I could feel my heartbeat increasing as the adrenalin started to rush through my body, causing me to feel extremely hot. What happened next was to startle me further, for as he was about to continue, he stopped mid-sentence and started to comment on how hot he was starting to feel! He then returned his attention to me, saying that he must be picking up these sensations from me! "How does he know?!" I thought. He then calmed me down explaining that there was nothing to fear and that his only intention was to provide help and assistance by channelling our Guides and helpers in Spirit.

There was much for me to ponder over after the extraordinary events of that evening. I was filled with two contrasting feelings. One was of apprehension and reservation, whilst the other was of exhilaration and excitement at the possibility that there really was something more beyond our normal senses. The subject that initially fascinated me the most promoted by this organisation, was the ability of healing and I subsequently became a regular visitor to their public library, pouring over the wealth of amazing information I found therein. At last I had found people practicing the miracle of healing!
Other times would find me 'picking the brains' of some of the resident Mediums and Healers in attendance. They explained some of the basic principles of healing and further indicated that I too could become a healer and all that was required of me, was a willing-ness to be an instrument for those in Spirit, generally referred to as Guides, to work through me. It was explained that these Guides are often highly advanced beings, that have learnt to utilise and direct energies that are not normally perceived or even understood by those of us in the physical plane and can affect the most amazing cures. It was further explained to me that the main concern of those that affect these cures, are more directed towards healing the cause of the various ailments, rather than their resultant physical manifestations, being that all things originate from Spirit. Several opportunities came my way to explore my own healing abilities. One of these was an elderly lady who suffered from continuous back pain and needed a

support frame to enable her to walk about. After a couple of sessions, she found that the pain eased considerably, allowing her to be less dependant on the frame.

Another occasion that springs to mind was again a back problem, this time it was a gentleman and I had to be extremely tactful in effecting a treatment, due to the high degree of scepticism that he had expressed regarding anything Supernatural or Paranormal. I told him that I may be able to ease his pain and got him to sit on a stool, close his eyes and relax. He was under the impression I was going to use some kind of massage technique, but as I stood behind him, I placed my hands about four inches away from his body and moved them up and down his back, calling on assistance from Spirit. Very soon I felt a warmth radiating from my hands and took this be to be the healing energy. When I finished he told me his back pain had been considerably relieved and then to my astonishment, he asked me what it was that I had pressed up against his spine that felt like a metal rod! Imagine his surprise when I told him that I had not even touched his back!

There were to be many other surprises in store for me as I explored this newly found ability further. One of these pertained to be my first experience of absent healing. It had been explained to me that the kind of healing I was learning was not faith healing, which, as the name implies, required the person's own faith to assist and effect the cure. What I was utilising was generally referred to as Spiritual Healing, and did not require any of the above. In fact the person need not even be consciously aware of it taking place at all, and furthermore it could be transmitted to them in their absence, hence the name. The occasion in question occurred when a friend of mine, informed me that his six-year-old niece had been admitted to hospital after discovering that she had a hole in the heart. The hospital informed the parents that they could operate, but due to other complications, there was a high risk that she may be partially paralysed for life. This caused me considerably distress, for I had enjoyed many delightful moments with this child, who was such a vibrant, lively and endearing young soul and the thought of her becoming paralysed was too much to bear. Then it occurred to me, "Why not try this absent healing" I thought. So summoning the assistance of my girlfriend Ingrid, we sent out our healing thoughts to the child. Several weeks later my friend approached me, asking whether I had been up to anything as the Doctors and Surgeons had become completely baffled by the discovery that the child no longer had any of the symptoms they had previously diagnosed and she was completely cured! You can imagine the joy and delight I experienced on hearing this news and it further made me realise that miracles do happen!

The summer season finally came to a close and I had made enquiries at a small privately owned holiday park, regarding setting up my own small portrait studio for the following summer season. I had quickly figured out that I could charge the same price as at *Butlins*, but instead of earning 50p per portrait, I could practically double my income by making my own frames and paying the camp 50p per portrait as their commission. I would further allow half an hour instead of twenty minutes for each sitting. In the meantime however, as of that moment, I was out of a job.

This situation fortunately was only temporary, as my girlfriend who had obtained employment at *Harrods* (the biggest department store in Knightsbridge, London) informed me that they were looking for more staff during the three months leading up to Christmas. I applied for a job in their Music Department and was accepted. My friend Mike also got a job with them and we shared a little bed-sit in Ladbroke Grove, just around the corner from the famous Portobello Road. I was excited to be in the 'Big City' and had great fun listening to all the latest music for sale in my department. Bands like *Santana*, *Emerson Lake and Palmer* and *Deep Purple* singing *Sweet Child of Time*, were among my favourites. I was a little bit worried by some of the other sales assistants in my department, as they were mostly 'gay' and they would continually tease and flirt with me. However I soon got used to this as it was only meant to be light-hearted fun and I did not feel offended, in fact some of them became really good friends and because most of them were involved in various capacities within the theatre, I got free invites for myself and Ingrid to a number of shows they were in, which was great fun.

After Christmas when the job ceased, I decided to stay on in the bed-sit in London and attempted to try and earn a living from going door to door offering my services as a Portrait Artist. This proved to be a bit of a gruelling period, as I tramped up and down the streets, knocking on doors in the bitter cold and damp, often without much success and ended up catching influenza. This turned out to be a blessing in disguise in some respects due to a rather unusual occurrence. I had very little money left and could not therefore afford to keep the only form of heating going in the bed-sit, which consisted of an electric fire operated by a meter that had to be continually fed with coins. Without heating, the room was freezing and damp. I only had enough money left to last an hour. I put the last of my coinage in to the meter and collapsed into bed feeling like death. I felt thoroughly miserable, lonely and wretched. My only comfort was a small portable cassette player and my favourite album at this time was *All Things Must Pass* by George Harrison, which featured the famous track called *My Sweet Lord*. As I lay there expecting the fire to go out at any moment, I called out to the Spirit realm and asked for help and healing. I was laid up in bed for three days and during this whole time the fire stayed on and never went out! Once again, I experienced another miracle!

After recovering, I made one more attempt at pursuing an income from my portraits, this time by setting myself up alongside Bayswater Road near Hyde Park, which was an established and well-known area of display for a number of varied Artists promoting their paintings and creations. I did moderately well for a short period of time in spite of the cold, however I soon became disenchanted and decided to go back home to my parents in Bognor. Soon was to begin another new chapter in my life.

## Chapter Eight: All that Glitters is Not Gold

Shortly after my return home to Bognor, my girlfriend Ingrid and I decided to get married. We found a fiat overlooking the sea and I spent the summer of 1971 drawing portraits at a private holiday camp at Bracklesham Bay where I had managed to set up my own studio, which was a great success. Shortly before the close of the summer season, my Dad (who was now permanently resident in the UK) had been introduced to a potential business opportunity that he had been informed could earn a generous income on a part time basis.

The company was called *Golden Products* and they produced a wide range of household cleaning products that were biodegradable and environmentally friendly. The company worked on a direct-to-consumer basis, which cut out the necessity of needing any premises to operate from, thus enabling more money to be spent on producing a high quality product, with greater profits being shared amongst it's Agents and Distributors who operated as self employed. The system that the company operated on was referred to as 'Pyramid Selling' or 'Multi-Level Marketing', which is similar to the method that a number of well-known and established companies like *Avon* and *Tupperware* utilise. In the *Golden Product's* operational structure, they had at the top of the pyramid those known as General Distributors, who could have any number of Direct Distributors below them (whom as the title implies purchase the products direct from the factory). One could buy oneself into this position by purchasing enough products to supply five Area Distributors who were next in the pyramid system, and one could buy oneself into this position by purchasing enough products to supply a team of Local Distributors, who formed the base of the pyramid system. The Local Distributors were supplied with a basic kit that would enable them to demonstrate the products, either by going door to door or by holding party plans. The only way one could become a General Distributor, sitting at the top of the pyramid, was by replacing oneself with another Direct Distributor. The company would then pay the General Distributor a bonus of £600. Unfortunately this was to become the eventual downfall of the company, as the focus became increasingly centred on the attainment of these bonuses, rather than the selling of the product. My Dad bought himself into the Direct Distributor position but soon discovered that he had no spare time to operate the business, due to being asked to set up a small airline service to the Channel Islands. As I was soon to be out of a job with the closing of the Summer season, I offered to take over the business from my Dad. The company's operations were designed to be ideally suited for a husband and wife team, so Ingrid and I were very excited at the potential prospects ahead of us.

One of the services provided by the company, was regular introduction meetings held at high profile hotels around the country, where the Distributors could invite prospective guests in order to introduce them to the company and build up one's own personal team. Regular training meetings were also provided.

When a Direct Distributor moves up to the position of General Distributor by replacing themselves, not only do they receive the £600 bonus but they are also sent (with their partner) to some exotic location abroad and put up in a luxurious hotel to spend a week being taught the secrets of becoming wealthy and successful by a team of Millionaires.

After about a month of being involved with the company, we had befriended an elderly single lady who was about to move up to the General position, which qualified her for the next training trip abroad which was to be held in Florida USA. As she did not have a partner to accompany her, she offered me the ticket. In no time at all, I was winging my way across the ocean on my way to Florida. It was a fascinating experience, meeting other Distributors from all over the world and sharing a common goal. One of the main ingredients for success that was constantly put forward by the companies wealthy representatives, was 'positive thinking', and furthered by the idea that by thinking and adopting an attitude of being successful and wealthy, one would attract the same towards oneself. Little did I realise until much later, that I was being subtly brainwashed. The whole experience was overlaid with an evangelistic fervour, not to mention mass indoctrination. During one of the sessions, one of the Speakers explained that the introductory meetings that were held for the benefit of recruiting new Distributors, were designed to take a person from a state of zero interest to the point where they would do anything to join. He further went on to explain that they had adopted the technique of achieving this from the famous evangelist Billy Graham, who in turn, had adopted the technique from the Communist Chinese for converting individuals to their ideals. The basic premise of this technique is based on the idea that generally, people do not make decisions on logic and reason alone, but that their emotions are the main factor.

This is how it was explained to me:-

A prospective client, who at this point may only be vaguely curious, is addressed by the Speaker, who introduces him/herself, and gives a little bit of background history. This part of the session is referred to as 'Identification' and is intended to invoke feelings of "Oh, they are just like me". This relaxes the prospective client. Next a little bit of logic and reason are presented to invoke the feeling of "That makes sense". Then comes the main key part of the technique which involves the speaker attacking himself e.g., "I struggled for years, trying to make ends meet and provide a quality life for my family, having to borrow money" etc - or in the case of Billy Graham; "I was a sinner, I used to drink, fornicate" etc... This part of the technique was to induce the feeling of "I'm in trouble!". Of course the final part of the technique was the 'SOLUTION', as in, "Join the company and fulfill all your dreams" - or in the case of Billy Graham; "Join with Jesus, let him save you".

It is curious recounting this episode in my life as to how oblivious I was that this very same technique, whilst being explained to us, was also being *used* on us! I have however no regrets, for I have learnt that all experiences, regardless of the form they take, are powerful teachers and regarding my involvement with *Golden Products* - I met some wonderful people and made some very dear friends.

On my return home from Florida I was bursting with enthusiasm - I felt I could take on the whole world. I was on a mission! In a brief span of time I had recruited a number of individuals as Area Distributors and set about the task of training them. My involvement with *Golden Products* lasted two years and was certainly a mixed bag of experiences. Due to my natural enthusiasm and positive outlook, which was one of the main ingredients for success that the company would encourage at the training sessions, I was asked to run the meetings and training sessions that were held at the *Metropole Hotel* in Brighton. I had been encouraged by the company to cut my hair (I must have been keen!), splash out on an expensive suit and take out a Hire Purchase Loan on a new car (an Opel Manta Sports Coupe). All this - just to give an impression of a 'successful business man'.

The fact that I wasn't earning much money at all was overcome by the continual encouragement and positive thinking process, advocated in the training programmes. It came as a great shock to me to find out that most of the Distributors sharing the running of the meetings and training programmes whom I thought to be really successful, were all in the same boat as me! Most were living off loans. There were however, other individuals earning large sums of money by taking advantage of the bonus scheme and who were introducing five to ten people a week to join the company, encouraging them to take out loans (secured on their properties), buying into the direct position, replacing themselves and then moving up to Generals and earning the Distributor position that introduced them £600 on each one. Unfortunately, most of those that were operating totally on the bonus scheme spent very little, or in most cases no time at all, assisting or training those people that they had introduced. Hardly any one was focusing on selling the product. I thought the products were excellent, furthermore, the fact that they were non-polluting was a big plus from my point of view, particularly as there was already a lot of information regularly featured in most of the national newspapers and on the TV news regarding the pollution in our lakes and rivers caused by domestic household cleaning products. I went the other extreme and practically became a nurse maid to my team of Distributors and whilst I wasn't adverse to taking advantage of the bonus scheme, I often felt uncomfortable about encouraging prospective agents to take out loans on the security of their homes, for I had witnessed the struggle of those that had already done this. I was not therefore, very successful in this particular area of activity.

By the second year of my involvement with the company, Ingrid and I had moved into a small luxury flat in Hove, just down the road from Brighton. I must admit that whilst we were not earning much money, we had great fun driving around the country in our new car, meeting loads of new people and being spurred on by our 'Golden' dream. Then towards the latter part of our second year in 1973, the bubble burst. Adverse publicity in the media, regarding companies enticing people into joining and using bonus schemes, came under scrutiny. We had just introduced an enthusiastic individual into the company and he was just about to move up into the General position, which would award us our first £600 (and we surely needed it!), when it was announced that earning bonuses from introductions was banned by the Government! On top of this, I got caught for speeding (for a third time) and got banned from driving for six months. Then it was, that Ingrid announced that she was pregnant!

We had to give up our flat as the tenancy disallowed children, which we found to be the general case elsewhere, and we eventually ended up lodging with my parents in Pagham, which was miles from Brighton. I carried on travelling to and fro, conducting meetings at the hotel in Brighton and often had to borrow money from my Mum for my train fare. In between this, I went out on my bike, knocking on doors trying to organise party plans in order to sell our stock of products. At this point, I decided to write to the company head office. I outlined my predicament and asked if they could provide some expenses so that I could continue running the meetings and training sessions. The company did not even bother to send me a reply. I was completely demoralised, disillusioned and despondent. I immediately quit the company. Very soon another new dimension was to enter my life.

## Chapter Nine: All Change

On July 30th 1973, Ingrid gave birth to twins - a girl and a boy, whom we named Carly and Marc. We had still been unable to find rented accommodation and after several months of staying with my parents, Ingrid decided to move into her Mother's flat with the twins in order to get on the Council House list. The flat wasn't big enough to accommodate all of us, so I had to rent a room elsewhere. I got a job as a Postman, which was convenient from the point of view that I finished work at midday, enabling me to spend time with the twins in the afternoon. It was a very strange predicament to be in, saying farewell to my wife and family as the evening came and going back to a lonely room on my own. It was quite a distressing time.

Three months passed by, then one day I got a call from a colleague who had worked as an Artist at *Butlins* with me years earlier, asking me if I would be interested in doing portraits for a Summer season at *Butlins* in Scarborough, Yorkshire. Normally I would not have entertained moving up to Yorkshire for the Summer had I been living with my family, but as I wasn't, I decided that it would be a good opportunity to earn some reasonable money.

Although I missed my family, I did find some things to delight in during this period away. I enjoyed the scenic sights of Scarborough and started writing songs again. I initially shared a cottage with some of the other Artists, which was great fun and we shared the same taste in music. Our favourite band was *Yes* and we continually played the track *Starship Trooper* at full volume - it was inspiring stuff. Two days after my return home from the Summer season in Yorkshire, a Council House came up and we were able to live as a family at last. I found myself a full time job working in a music shop and befriended another Musician working there and we started writing songs together.

At this point in my life, I had already become a Vegetarian and was contemplating becoming a Vegan. This decision was motivated partly by the cruelty I was made aware of that existed in the factory farming systems. I have always loved animals and I no longer wished to be a party to their unnecessary suffering just to feed me, especially as I had been made aware of alternative food sources. The other factor that determined my decision came about after reading an article on the potential introduction of eating horse meat (as is done on the continent) due to a meat shortage that Britain was experiencing at the time. I was so incensed and outraged by the idea that I suddenly had to question myself as to why I was so upset about eating horses but not concerned about eating cows or sheep! I further remembered that when I lived in Borneo, it was common for the local folk to eat dog meat, the thought of which would probably upset most people here in England as it did me. From that point on to this day I never ate meat again.

I worked at the music shop for six months during the Winter and saved enough money to buy a really nice acoustic guitar (which I still use to this days). I also continued my exploration of the world of Spiritual Healing and deepened my understanding of contact with the consciousness that inhabits the Spirit realms. It was revealed to me that everything in existence contains consciousness, and that the ability that is referred to as our 'psychic' or 'intuitive' senses, is the means by which we are able to communicate with them. This ability is not just for a chosen few - everybody has the potential to develop these senses as they are an inherent natural part of our overall being. Some people's abilities are more prominent than others, only to the same extent that some individuals might display a naturally artistic or musical ability.

Having been made aware that physical death is not the end of us and that the consciousness that is our true being moves on to another plane of existence, I was finding myself continually pondering over what these other planes of existence were like. I mean, how do they spend their day?!

A few weeks later I was strolling around the shops in Brighton doing a bit of window shopping. My thoughts couldn't have been further away from the above subject matter. I found myself wandering into a large bookshop and randomly bent down and picked a book off the shelf (as you do). The title of the book was *Life in the World Unseen* by Anthony Borgia. I turned it over to read the back introduction. This was the story of a Catholic Priest who had a natural Psychic gift, which at first he considered to be a gift from God. However when he discussed this gift with his superiors, they convinced him that it was the Devil's work and subsequently indoctrinated him into believing that the Psychic gift was evil, so much so that he eventually wrote a number of damning books on the subject, discouraging anyone from developing these abilities or attempting to communicate with those in Spirit. Then, he died. The book is an in-depth outline of what he experienced immediately on passing over after he died; whom he was greeted by, where he went, and the immense variety of realms he was shown. He was immediately overcome with remorse at how misguided he had become during his earth life regarding the communication with Spirit. Realising that it was far from being the Devil's work, he subsequently requested that he could write a book from Spirit in order to rectify the errors he committed during his lifetime. Permission was granted for him to utilise the services of a Medium that could channel the book for him. I was astounded at how I had seemingly randomly picked this book off the shelf (out of all the books in the store), which held answers to the many questions I had been pondering regarding life in the Spirit realms. Coincidence or synchronicity?

By spring 1974 I finished working at the music shop and set up my own portrait studio again, this time at *Pontins Holiday Camp* at Camber Sands, Sussex. I was to maintain this concession for the next five years. It was a most intriguing and interesting period of time. I was to discover that for some inexplicable reason (which I understand now), many people who came for a portrait sitting (mostly women and children), would start to relate a variety of different Psychic experiences - out of body experiences being the most common - and naturally these folk were very often quite frightened and disturbed by them. Even stranger was that they did not know why they were telling me, other than they felt I would understand. In most cases they had not even told their partners for fear of being ridiculed! Yet, somehow they felt comfortable with telling me! As I was exploring and studying the subject, I was able to put their minds at rest by explaining many of the phenomena they were experiencing. Yet more phenomena… or synchronicities?

A little later on, I was down at the local Spiritualist Church pouring through their library books and decided to sit in on a session that was occurring next door. The visiting Medium randomly addressed and gave messages to various individuals, then directed her attention towards me. What she said was quite startling in light of the above. She said that I talk to a lot of people about this subject - I answered affirmative - she then went on to ask if it ever occurred to me that some people might think that I was a bit "loopy?". "No!" I answered, and this was true, I had never really considered that. She continued saying "Great, keep up the good work, as Spirit is working through you as a channel and guiding you in what you say!".

This was for me most exciting, and confirmed a number of extraordinary things. For instance, I would often be asked questions relating to this topic that I had no idea how to answer - then suddenly into my mind would pop a simple analogy that would perfectly explain and answer the question, more often than not, I would be surprised by this as well. Since that time, I have recognised that the source of the foundations for most of my own understanding of Spirit, has actually been uttered from my own mouth!

During this period at the holiday camp I became involved with several of the resident bands and wrote some songs both for and with them. One particular band I got involved with named *Gold*, were invited to do a tour of Russia. This was during the time that Russia was just starting to open up to western pop music. Elton John had just completed a tour prior to *Gold's* arrival. Thinking that *Gold* were a famous UK band, the Russians gave them the same red carpet treatment and reception they had given Elton John! Whilst over there, the band produced a live album which included one of my songs called *Midnight Light*. They were seen on TV by millions of viewers and the album sales were over a quarter of a million. "Fantastic!" I thought, considering my share of the royalties (which I worked out to be at least £50,000). I then did a very foolish thing. At the time I was suffering a bit financially and on the strength of the above news, I took out a loan. Then came the bombshell. Because Russia is a Communist state and the record company was state owned, they would not pay out a single penny (or rouble) in royalties. Imagine how devastated I was - especially as I now had a loan to pay back too. To make matters worse, another song I co-wrote with *Gold* suffered a different but no less painful fate. The song in question was a powerful emotive ballad entitled *This Woman*, which we played to one of the regular performers who did the *Pontins* cabaret circuit - a lady called Iris Williams (undiscovered at that time). Her style was very much in the style of Shirley Bassey. Iris Williams absolutely loved the song! So much so that she got her Manager to organise a studio recording of it. She performed this song regularly and even performed it when she did a tour of Australia. Then disaster struck - I had noticed on a number of occasions that the attitude of the band members of *Gold* was frequently bordering on arrogance, particularly towards the general public. I often used to comment on this. Due to this attitude, they eventually got into conflict with Iris Williams and her Manager, to the extent that they dropped the song and did not want anything more to do with the band. The following year, Iris Williams got to number one in the charts with a song entitled *He Was Oh So Beautiful*, and she went on to become a successful international artist. I was gutted, as she would have most certainly included our track on one of her albums - it may even have been a single as she loved it so much!

I was now feeling decidedly unhappy about my association with *Gold* - then came the final straw. During the following Winter months, I set up my new portrait studio in a Department store in Brighton. A dear elderly lady commissioned me to draw a portrait of a German Shepherd (Alsatian) dog as a Christmas present for a friend. I offered to deliver it for her on my way home and discovered that she lived in a plush luxury apartment on the seafront in Hove. When I went into her lounge, I spied a large grand piano sitting in the middle of the room. The conversation immediately turned to music, and I told her I was a Songwriter. She immediately asked me if I had anything on tape and I told her the only piece of music I had was the Iris Williams song, which I gave her. Unbeknown to me at that point, was that the friend for whom I had drawn the portrait of the Alsatian (and who lived next door) was in fact a top music Producer and Publisher - in fact he used to manage Shirley Bassey! Imagine my surprise when I received a telephone call from him informing me that he loved the song and furthermore wanted to publish it! He went on to say that he had a number of Artists in the same class as Shirley Bassey, who would most certainly love to perform the song. This was great! He further explained that he understood the song was co-written and that he would need permission from the other co-writers. I eagerly gave him the contact number for *Gold*. One week passed, then two, then finally I received the call. What a disappointment. "I am sorry Nick" he said, and then went on to explain that he could not do anything with the song as he did not want to have anything to do with the other co-writers as they were so rude to his partner! "Oh no"! I thought, "not again"! This was a real blow, and I plummeted into a deep despondency.

By 1975 after a great deal of soul searching, I decided that trying to write commercial music was just not happening. It was then that I decided to marry my music with my Spiritual path. Recognising the beneficial healing potency of music, I threw myself wholeheartedly into this endeavour, even though I knew this to be a harder path to follow. At this particular point in time, I was aware of only one other Musician pursuing this path. Having been inspired by the growing 'New Age' movement, I decided to call my music 'New Age Music' (this was long before it became an established category). One of the other things I decided was that I was no longer going to rely on other bands to perform my music, so I formed my own band. I originally named the band *Lightwave*, then *Starwave* and eventually settled on *Pegasus*.

I referred to the band's music as 'New Age Rock Music' and we performed at one of the earliest *Mind Body Spirit* exhibitions at Earls Court, London (I still attend many of their exhibitions to this day).

During our performance I met a well-known Crystal Healer named Ra Bonewitz. I had not been aware of crystal energies at all up to this point and was fascinated by his explanations.

He explained that he used to work as a Geophysicist in America and understood both the scientific and Spiritual applications of crystal energy. He donated a large beautiful Quartz crystal to the band, further explaining that crystals not only store energy but that they also boost energy, and he advised that we use it as an additional amplifier whenever we rehearsed or performed. Ra further told me that his wife was a well-known Astrologer and wrote a column in a national newspaper. She had recently approached *Polydor Records* and was producing a series of astrological readings on vinyl disc. Before I knew it, I was recording a demo of one of my songs in their studio! This was wonderful, or so I thought. Shortly after this, I received a call from Ra informing me that the record company liked the song, however they wanted me to make a few changes. Firstly they wanted me to get rid of the Singer and find a new one, and secondly they wanted me to change some of the lyrics. The song in question was entitled *Starchild* and the story line was about a female extraterrestrial that came to assist humanity. The record company wanted to change it to a male, as they thought it would be good to tie it in with Christmas. In other words the inference would relate it to Jesus being the Starchild. Now I do not have any qualms about Jesus at all, however this was not what the song was about at all. This started to make me think how many other compromises they were going to impose on me. I was most certainly not going to just 'dump' our Singer on their say so, especially after all the hard work she had put into the band - this was just not on! So as painful as it was to do, I said "No deal". Thus ended Pegasus. Also, thus ended my marriage to Ingrid, which had been under considerable strain for a while.

I entered a dark and dismal period in my life. During this time I was reminded of how much I had admired those Songwriters who had suffered and from their pain had written such inspiring works and how I had wished to know that kind of suffering. Careful of what you ask for - you might just get it!

How miserable I felt, especially being parted from my children, who now numbered three, as apart from the twins we now had another beautiful daughter - Anna Celeste - who was now two years old. I love my children, who have always been a great source of joy in my life and I have always played an active role in their upbringing. I was the one who told them stories and tucked them in at night. I can recall one particular amusing incident one night after I had just tucked them in. After saying goodnight to them, I would always look out of the window and stare up at the night sky. My children would ask me what I was doing and my reply would be "Looking for flying saucers". On this particular occasion, my son Marc (who was about six years old at the time) piped up and said, "How come flying saucers never come down our street Daddy?!". This still amuses me to this day.

After I moved out, I initially stayed with friends from the band and then moved into a small bed-sit with only a small electric fire for heating (and Winter was just around the corner)! It was very grim and I remember when the twins came to visit me, my daughter Carly said to me, "This room doesn't suit you Daddy"! Seeing my children and the belief that my music was important, were the only things that kept me going at that time. By Christmas I was in a sorry state, having had a brief relationship with another lady that ended on Christmas Eve. I felt totally alone. I remember wandering around the shops in the evening and looking into the TV shop window and one of my favourite programmes - *Star Trek* - was showing, but not even this raised my Spirits. Funny how things that one is used to, and even finds comfort in, can be so totally devoid of meaning when things change. Our state of mind tends to prioritise the various elements that make up our daily lives. All the time we seem to get caught up in the things that seem so important at the time and then, in a blink of an eye, they are gone!

When I got home, I received a call from my ex-wife inviting me for Christmas lunch with the children, which I thought was very kind of her and lifted my Spirits considerably. Come New Years Eve, a close friend who was the Keyboard Player in my band named Skot, placed a tape in my hand. He had overlaid some keyboard tracks over one of our songs called *Ascent*, that we had recorded during one of our rehearsals. It was ecstatic and really lifted my Spirits. It was such an uplifting piece of music. What a lovely gift he had given me for the New Year! New hope stirred within me. I don't know how many times I played that tape - but suffice to say that it did the trick. It lifted me out of my depression and confirmed the powerful healing qualities of music. I started writing more new songs that lifted me out of my despair - music that healed me!

I paused to wonder on what had taken place in my life at this point. Had I created all this suffering as a result of a fixed belief? I recalled how I had admired all those Songwriters who created such inspiring musical works as a result of their suffering and I found myself asking whether it is necessary to suffer in order to create inspiration. How often is it expressed that some of our greatest good has come from a bad situation? Is it necessary for there to be some 'bad' in order to generate some 'good'? I also found myself wondering how things would be if we moved out of the continual concept of the good versus bad scenario.

We are continually faced daily with being told "This is good for you, this is bad for you". What would happen if we moved out of judgment - what then? Well, one could exercise one's freedom to choose, after all, is not belief based on choice? On other words, whatever one *chooses* to believe. If we explore this further, one choice we could make by moving out of the good/bad scenario could be to accept that everything just *is*, and therefore do whatever we want. To do whatever you want implies the use of free will, and don't all major Religions and Spiritual teachings advocate the gift of free will? So what exactly is free will? One could say that the choice to view things in a particular way, be it positive or negative, is exercising free will. Is it though? Because either choice could be loaded with and coloured by previous experiences or perhaps even conditioned programmed responses.

The view that one upholds at any given moment could be tainted with a million undetected, unsuspected or unexamined mixtures of real knowledge mixed with hearsay. How often do we generally accept and propagate knowledge from experiences that come second hand from close friends, family or people we admire? This will of course be dependant on our opinions or even judgements that we have of the value of their opinions (this is a mine-field!). How many times if one is honest, do we just accept without question, the opinions or views of particular individuals that we admire? How often is a speculative idea from such an individual taken or accepted as fact? Often this information gets shared - passed on by word of mouth, each adding their own little opinion or version (Chinese Whispers!). Now try to unravel this lot within your own circle of friends, family and work colleagues - then multiply it by all the people in the world! Good grief - talk about overload! So have you ever felt you're going mad? How do we manage to stay sane? Are we ever in fact sane? What is sanity anyway? Surely the answer will depend on one's viewpoint? Which brings us back to choices - and what was choice about? Free Will?

Well what do we do?…Another choice could be to just *accept* that all things (regardless of good, bad, right, wrong etc) are 'valid'. That would fit with everything just being 'is'. Is this just another chosen belief? Yes. Is it a 'knowing'?…Does it matter?…Let's keep going with it being a choice  - a chosen belief. If we *choose* to view that all things are valid, this could be equated to all things having equal value. How would we conduct our lives if this were so? Well it would be pointless to try and *be better* than anyone else. Are there not countless manifestations of a need, addiction or obsession with trying to raise ourselves up - to be looked up to? (Often a reaction to being looked 'down upon' or 'put down'). Have you ever experienced being looked down on or put down? Yes? No? Did your parents (bless them) ever put you down? Brothers, sisters, schoolmates, teachers, work colleagues, bosses or society?…

Let's go back to all things being valid or equal. If what one does is no more important than anything else why bother? Perhaps one could forget trying to be important (doesn't feel comfortable does it)? How about reversing it and recognising that *everything* is important - that way one could enjoy feeling as important as one likes at the same time as enjoying how everyone else feels important! Hmm, maybe! This won't work if one's interpretation of importance is based on the 'need' to be more important than others i.e., Superior, and therefore having power over others.

Being in Charge. Being in Control. Oh yes we want that don't we? Or do we? Where does this need actually spring from? What of media and advertising? We are continually fed images of lifestyles, cars, houses, clothes, products, hi-fi's etc that are the 'best'…and of course you've got to have the 'best' to impress. Impress whom? Girlfriends, boyfriends, parents, brothers, sisters, work colleagues - and then they'll look up to us won't they? Well…some might, on the other hand, some might be quite indifferent (cross them off the Christmas Card List)!
Hmm! What are we getting into here, motives? Intents and hidden agendas, group subconscious suppressed emotions? Some individuals even *choose* to be inferior as well - what effect does this create? If based on lack of self-worth, it could result in others feeling sorry for us - that gives us attention, gets us

'noticed' - gives an excuse not to get involved - pushes others away - gives one space. Being superior gets attention too, of a different kind. Some want to be the focus of attention. Is this based on a 'need to receive' from others? Or is it a 'take' from others. What is the difference? Well, to receive from others generally implies that the other party has given consent of their own free will to 'give. To take is the reverse - often it can be an imposition or invasion of another's personal space, belongings etc. Are these the kind of scenarios witnessed daily and sent as visual images around the world on TV or read about in newspapers?

And what is our view of 'love'? When we love somebody do we give our love freely, unconditionally, do we receive it freely or do we ever demand it or take it? Do we ever 'withhold' it? Do we create 'conditions' for the giving or receiving! I think most would say that if they were really honest, there is a little bit of each in there. Would it be fair to say as a general understanding that most individuals *desire* to be loved? Where exactly does the desire to be loved stem from? Is it insecurity? The need to be secure in being a part of something or someone, the need to belong, be needed, cared for, to care, the need to give, to feel special even superior? All this boils down to choices regarding the way we are viewing our experiences in life at any given moment. It is also dependant on intentions or motives regarding the same.

Another choice could be based on preferences rather than judgments. How would this work if one is offered or experiences something that genuinely distresses us? We could *choose* to see it as having validity but *prefer* (from choice) a different experience (and not experience it at all). Or one could choose to *embrace* or *allow* the experience and decide (choose) that it has a beneficial outcome. After all, what is reality and what is illusion? Perhaps they occupy the same space (more paradoxes). Perhaps good, bad, right, wrong, love and hate all occupy the same space?

Are we creating realities that perpetuate 'separation'? Or do we choose to create realities that create 'wholeness', linking together i.e., uniting and integrating? The question is: What does one want? What choice to make?

So back to the story…

The year was 1982 and what I really wanted at this time was a job and the creation of a new life. A new partner named Tahnee came into my life and I was renewed and inspired. I continued to explore my Spiritual interests, which were now linking even more with the UFO phenomena - I was starting to see a connection. All manner of bizarre information was coming to light. I finally got a job with a music copyright company, and within three years I had worked my way up to a higher position in the company, which was negotiating and issuing licenses for use of music in films and TV commercials etc.

I was now living in Croydon, Surrey. I bought myself a keyboard and learnt to play it by composing new songs. This was an immensely creative and productive period in many ways. New inspiring songs were just pouring out of me. My interest in UFO's continued and now Crop Circles were coming into the picture. I went to the local library and digested as much information on these topics as I could, trying to form a picture of what was 'really' happening.

Some of these books were factual accounts of individual's personal experiences, some of them were channelled sources. One particular book intrigued me, as I became aware that around the world only ten countries officially recognised UFO's as a genuine phenomenon. England and America are not one of these, and both these countries plus many others have 'D' notices on this information, which is a classified restriction imposed by the Governments disallowing any significant information on UFO's being disclosed in the general media. "Why?" I asked myself. However, the book I stumbled upon was a French publication and France is one of the ten countries that do officially recognise UFO's. The book contained extracts from a popular radio show that invited individuals from all walks of life to talk about their personal experiences. These ranged from simple farm folk to police and pilots. I was very surprised to discover an interview with Professor Hynek, a Scientific Advisor for the American *Project Blue Book,* an official body that was set up to research UFO phenomena. The resultant conclusion of this investigator organisation was that there was nothing of significance to be found! Professor Hynek was also the Consultant Scientist for the film *Close Encounters of the Third Kind.* What was really interesting and intriguing was his remarks as to how disgusted he was with the conclusions of *Project Blue Book* in the light of the immense and overwhelming genuine data regarding UFO's.

I also started to subscribe to an alternative magazine published by the *Theosophical Society*, called *Viewpoint Aquarius*, which regularly contained accounts of UFO experiences from around the world - it was mind boggling! It also contained information on the *Philadelphia Experiment* that was supposed to have taken place in 1943 (the same time as the term 'flying saucers' appeared). The story goes that using alien technology, the US navy teleported the ship *USS Eldridge* from one dock to another. The ship remained intact but the crew suffered terribly, some merged embedded in the ship, others dematerialised. The resulting experiment had literally torn a 'rip' in the fabric of time - they had created a 'time tunnel'! This story continues with further experiments using Psychics linked to computers, some of which involved mind control experiments. These further experiments were meant to have taken place at Montauk on Long Island, USA. Fact or fiction? Who knows for sure but something was afoot.

On the basis that there may be some truth to it, particularly regarding 'official conspiracies', what could *I* as an individual do about it? Well I could focus positive energies to balance the scales a bit. I was even more determined to create healing and uplifting music as well. I chose to *believe* that the only real way to inspire others is by one's own example - in other words 'live' one's truth, whatever one perceives that to be - the Native Americans would call it "Walking the talk".

On the subject of truth, how can one really know if something is true? My personal view is that by practicing and living as 'true' as one can be, i.e., being truthful and true to *one's self*, creates a resonance and one instinctively knows and recognises it. I always felt this way when bringing up my children. I had observed many parents tell 'little white lies' to their kids, oftentimes because it was easier than trying to explain the truth to their enquiring young minds. I refused to do this. I wanted my children to grow up respecting truth and honesty and the only way they were going to experience this would be from their parents example. To me it is totally logical. *Live the truth and you shall know it*. I feel the same way about love - *Live love and you shall know it*.

So what of Crop Circles? The first reported circles appeared in a farmer's field down in Warminster in Wiltshire, England - near Cley Hill (so it was reported in the newspapers). I went with my partner Tahnee to view them first hand myself, spending an all night vigil searching for saucers. Unfortunately the farmer had ploughed the field by the time we got there - blast! One of my books had stated that Warminster was one of the most prolific areas for spotting UFO's. I didn't see any though, however my partner did - very briefly she saw some unusual light formations. Oh well, try again next year!

By 1986 I had become disenchanted with the copyright company I was working for and decided to leave and set up my own music label which I called *Wandering Minstrel Music*. I initially thought I might specialise in writing 'jingles' or to be more adventurous and get into writing film scores. Unfortunately this was a very 'closed shop', so instead I produced *The River Song Suite* - a collection of gentle acoustic guitar pieces, many of which I had composed over the years when frequenting the woods or sitting by the river or other natural surroundings, inspired by Nature.

The album was overlaid with a gentle healing quality and intent. Having produced this album entirely off my own back, I now had the job of marketing it! This was a new and daunting experience. I decided that the obvious place to start was in the 'New Age' market place. I had become aware that there were many New Age fayres, festivals and 'Green' fayres going on around the country. At this point in time a directory of New Age events did not exist so much information came from word of mouth.

During my first year marketing the album at numerous fayres and festivals, I made a lot of contacts and friends. The album was received enthusiastically and numerous Healers and healing centres used the album as a compliment to their therapies. I made contact with a number of New Age shops that stocked this album. Although the sales were not immense, it was still very encouraging. At the tail end of 1986 I met the renowned Healer Mathew Manning, an individual I had heard much about. He told me that he was setting up his own music label called *Cloud Nine* and wanted exclusive rights on *The River Song Suite*. I felt disinclined to give away those rights at this point and told him I would write an album specifically for his label. Thus my next album *Earthdance* was born - another instrumental album that was slightly more orchestrated than *The River Song Suite*.

I had already met a young man named Steve Jay who ran his own recording studio called *Merlyns Cave* and he had such lovely 'toys' to play with in the studio. He had a *Fairlight* computer - one of the first digital instruments that had banks of 'real' instrumental sounds programmed into it e.g., strings, choirs, pianos - you name it! I eagerly incorporated these sounds into *Earthdance*. This album was a celebration of the seasons of Nature and drew a parallel with the cycles of Spiritual growth;

Spring relating to birth/rebirth, Summer relating to experience, Autumn as a reflection of experience and Winter as an initiation - a period where on the surface, nothing appears to be going on but under the surface, deep within, a gestation and integration of all the above occurs, resulting in a transformation and finally a new re-birth onto another level, and harmonic with the previous knowledge and experiences of the first cycle. This process continues spiralling upwards. I went through a series of very trying personal experiences producing this album and it wouldn't be until at least 1993, when I recognised that I was literally creating and experiencing in my physical reality, the themes which I chose for each album!

## Chapter Ten: Myth and Magic

1988 was an extremely interesting year in that I was inspired by a book called *The Mists of Avalon* by Marion Bradley, a best seller that told an unusual version of the King Arthur legend as seen through the eyes of Morgaine Le Fey (often depicted as evil in traditional tales). Here however she was simply described as a dedicated Priestess who honoured both the Male and Female creator - the God and Goddess. She was of the old Religion known as Paganism, that honoured and respected Nature and celebrated the seasons by holding ceremonies at the solstices. I was soon to learn more of this particular belief system.

I had always been inspired by the legend of King Arthur legend and I found *The Mists of Avalon* highly provocative. I also 'got wind' that a TV production of the book was about to be produced. I eagerly started producing music for this! I was to entitle this album *Out of the Mist (The Quest for Avalon)*. I made contact with the TV company *HTV* based in Bristol who were the Co-Producers and submitted twenty minutes of music with the hope they may use it in the production. The response was positive, however they explained they had not even sorted the script out yet and music is usually always the last consideration in those kinds of productions. A couple of weeks later I was informed that *HTV* was no longer involved in the project. I tracked down the main Producers  *Pan Piper Productions* based in America - owned by the actor James Coburn. "How does one get hold of him?" I asked myself. Then a strange quirk of fate occurred…

On visiting Glastonbury on one of my own personal quests, I had picked up a local magazine, which I had tucked away when I got home and which had become buried under a pile of other magazines. During a clear out, I came across it and I was randomly glancing through it and came across a notice explaining that the writer of the *Mists of Avalon*, Marion Bradley, would be visiting England shortly and could be contacted through the shop *Gothic Image*. I eagerly contacted the shop as I knew the Manager Jamie George and explained my predicament. Jamie explained to me that he was a personal friend of Marion Bradley and would be only too pleased to pass my music cassette on to her. I was delighted to receive a positive response from her commenting on how much she really enjoyed the music but further explained that she did not have any involvement in the TV production. The best she could do was to forward the tape via her Agent, onto *Pan Piper Productions*. After a period of several months, I was informed that the production was no longer to go ahead and instead was shelved for the time being.

I was obviously a little disappointed at first, but was consoled with the fact that I had produced nearly half an album's worth of material, so I rapidly completed it. Here yet again occurred another intriguing co-incidence or perhaps synchronicity, for up until this point in time, most of the fayres and festivals I had performed and marketed my music at were New Age or Green Eco fayres. Through some new contacts I had made at some of these, I was suddenly introduced to the Pagan fayres - curious considering the theme of the new album! Suddenly I was thrust into this curious world, meeting Druids, Witches, Priests and Priestesses of the 'old Religion'. I had had very little understanding of their ways and had only really heard the general prejudiced views of how they are often portrayed.

I met a very mixed bag of interesting individuals, for the most part extremely genuine, although there were a few 'over the top' characters caught up a bit in the pomp and ceremony, not unlike those characters caught up in the pomp and ceremony of other extreme Religious groups. I had never felt particularly comfortable with some of the displays of overt ritual practices, regardless of who conducted them. I personally felt they distracted one from the simple gentle essence of the real genuine teachings.
It was incredible how many individuals I met that year that claimed they were the reincarnation of Merlin, King Arthur, Guinevere or Morgan Le Fey! It would have been very easy to dismiss these folk as crackpots, yet their sincerity was truly apparent - well okay,
some were a bit off the wall! I wasn't particularly perturbed by this as I felt it was quite possible (provided one chooses to accept reincarnation), that an entity or being renowned and celebrated from our early history, could very well choose to fragment itself and incarnate within several 'individuals'. After all, many Spiritual traditions speak of the original Creator God - or whatever name one chooses, splitting and fragmenting itself in order to create new experiences of itself. Perhaps this is the reason there are more people in the world today than in previous history! I continue to meet more and more individuals experiencing and connecting up with like minds. Perhaps this is the beginning of the return journey - all the tiny fragments that have been separated for so long, at last joining and re uniting, re-connecting, returning to the source - it could be! Furthermore

many Spiritual wisdoms comment on the 'illusion of separation', explaining that in reality nothing is separate and everything is interconnected - part of a whole.

Well here I was meeting all these colourful folk, talking to them about their Pagan belief which I found had a lot in common with the Native American teachings. I must admit that I felt a certain resonance with the simple principles of Paganism, for instance; I have always loved and honoured Nature and the planet Earth. I have always found the concept of an 'all male' God or Creator preposterous, when everything in Nature is male *and* female. So to me if there is to be a Creator it would have to encompass both essences.

During that summer of 1988, I was informed by a friend (another artist who lived in Glastonbury) that a new sword was being made for Avalon. It was to be made in the old tradition of ritual swords by a Master Druid and was to be used as a tool for 'cleansing' the energies at sacred sites like Stonehenge and Avebury, for it was felt that there had been a certain abuse and misuse of these ancient sites. I had been working on the album all year and by the Autumn I had completed it. I recorded the album at my friend's studio, which was now located by the Malvern Hills in Worcestershire, and I couldn't help but wonder at the synchronicity of writing this new album in a studio called *Merlyns Cave*!

I was also further surprised to discover that the Malvern Hills frequently feature in the Arthurian Legends and were known at that time as Dragon Island (more synchronicities?). I had also been made aware that in many traditions Merlin is symbolised by the number 8. Here I was celebrating the completion of the album on the 8/8/88! During this time of year in Malvern, they had a festival called *The Fringe* and a friend who organised the bands arranged a performance for me of my newly completed album. It was amazing! We played in a medieval style marque. A friend from *Starchild* (a shop in Glastonbury) came up and brought a load of incense to create a mist effect on stage (we had tried unsuccessfully to hire a smoke machine). I had written a narration to accompany each musical composition during the performance, which was read by a close friend named Jon Wadge, who dressed up as Merlin. We took a break halfway through the set and proceeded into the second half which opened with a dramatic fanfare track entitled *Bring Forth The Sword*. A few bars into the opening theme and 'lo and behold' who should appear walking out to the front of the stage but my

Artist friend from Glastonbury Peter Pracownik, holding the sword that had been specially made for Avalon! Accompanying him was a genuine Druid named Drew! He raised the sword aloft as the music peaked, honoured the four directions and then thrust it into the ground in front of the stage - it was perfect! I was utterly amazed as it was totally unexpected! Peter had heard I was going to perform the album but he had no idea of the music programme. He had spontaneously jumped in the car and had driven 80 miles up the motorway and had arrived at the perfect moment!

Synchronicity? Yes, I think so! It was a magical experience. So what would 1989 bring I wondered. Just before the final close of that year of 1988, having completed the album *Out of the Mist*, which at that time was a real highlight to me in terms of realising my creative ability to write, compose and produce a highly orchestrated piece of musical excellence. I suddenly felt at a complete loss as to what to create next. How was I to follow this one? I felt I had suddenly 'dried up' creatively. My friend Jon Wadge (who had played the part of Merlin) was staying with me at the time and he suddenly came out with an intriguing piece of channelling. Jon is a highly intuitive natural Psychic and Healer - although be does not consider himself as such (as is often the way with the real genuine article)! He told me not to worry about trying to come up with a new musical idea, instead he said I should get my pastels and paper out and over the next seven days draw one picture a day! "Just draw anything" he said, as he felt that something would come out of it. His conviction and the way he put this across made me take notice.

So I immediately set up my easel in readiness. I was to start the first picture the following day, however an urgent family matter arose that took me out for most of the day. I arrived back home at 11.45pm. I had totally forgotten about the picture until I went into my 'music room' and saw the easel waiting there. "Panic!" I thought!..." Wait a minute though...I've still got 15 minutes left of the day". So I quickly grabbed the pastels and scribbled random strokes across the paper, I did not even turn the light on - I had no idea what I was creating. I rubbed it all in then turned on the light. "Oh what a mess", was my immediate reaction, but on closer inspection, some interesting effects had taken place with the merging colours of the pastels. There was a little elfin face, a stags head and an angels wing. I was totally unaware that I could get such effects from pastels! I had only ever used them for drawing portraits and I had never really experimented with them. This inspired me greatly and the next day I took more time, working in the same way, randomly scribbling on the paper. After observing the result and perceiving any kind of 'accidental image', I immediately set about developing it. It was amazing to see the picture unfold before me without any preconceived notion of what I was to produce. Over the next seven days I was astounded by the results. Jon was right - something had come out of this. I had now added an extra new ability and dimension to my artistic talents. I now understood that Spirit wished to channel through me as a Psychic Artist! I was excited! Furthermore, I could now produce my own visual images for the covers of my musical albums...great!

## Chapter Eleven: Into the Fire

It was now 1989 - the beginning of another new year and another new album was in formation. Originally this new album was going to be entitled *Wings of Fire*. Unfortunately however, another musician I had met at a newly formed *New Age Music Association* (New Age music was starting to become an established area of music by now) was also going to call his album by the same name! Yet another synchronicity?

Furthermore (and this is even more bizarre), out of curiosity I asked him what image he was going to put on his album sleeve - his reply was an eagle descending from the sky with it's wings aflame! Exactly the same image that I had come up with for my album! As he had already arranged the printing of the labels for his album and mine had yet to be done, I decided to change the name of my album - hence *Into the Fire* was born and that is exactly where I went!!!

The concept for this album was to encapsulate my own astrological sun sign Sagittarius - a fire sign. I also wanted to pay a tribute to the Native American symbol for my sign, which in their tradition is the Thunderbird, hence one of the tracks on the album is called *Flight of the Thunderbird*. The first track written for this album was actually recorded on the Summer solstice and was entitled *Temple of the Sun*. This album was the most powerful and dynamic composition I had written up to that time and on playing it to a Medium friend I knew, she was immediately captivated by its power and felt it was ideal for meditative journeys. She subsequently still plays it regularly to her students in her development classes. (I have since changed the name of the album from *Into the Fire* to *Temple of the Sun*).

I was still faced with the need to satisfactorily market my albums and Mathew Manning had since folded up his *Cloud Nine* label due to personal reasons. I decided to take a big chance and to invest in myself. After reluctantly agreeing, my partner and I took a loan out on our flat and funded a two week trip to America. I had been given to understand that New Age Music was well established over there. One of my other hopes for this trip was the possibility of meeting some real Native Americans! Alas this was not the case. We eventually ended up just having a nice holiday after discovering on arrival to the States, that New Age Music was undergoing a radical change and several New Age Music labels were folding up. This was very disappointing and nothing transpired for promoting my music there at that time. Shortly after returning to England I was contacted by an ex-

Policeman friend, Ray Murray, who had been actively involved with the Japanese Buddhist monks, based at the Peace Pagoda in Milton Keynes (they also have one in Battersea, London).

I had been invited in previous years to perform my music at their 'Peace Ceremonies' and on this occasion Ray informed me that they wanted me to arrange a concert involving other New Age Musicians as well as myself. He explained further that the Japanese Monks were involved with a group of Native Americans who were reactivating the old tradition of the 'Sacred Run'. Running in relays, they were to run across America, fly over to England and stop over a few days at Milton Keynes, where the concert would take place. They would then run across Europe and end up in Russia. The Sacred Run tradition is a prayer for world peace - every step they take is honouring the Earth. I was amused by the fact that I had travelled all the way to America in the hope of meeting Native Americans and here I was meeting them in Milton Keynes of all places! Unfortunately this event did not get as much publicity as was hoped, due to the news being dominated by the Gulf War - how ironic.

The Gulf War had a very dramatic effect upon me, as I am sure it did for many others. Was this the fulfilment of the prophecies of the Third World War and the darkening of the skies? Horrific images were brought straight into one's home courtesy of network TV. I was also having a personal crisis of my own, for some strange reason. The creation of the *Into the Fire* album took a lot out of me. I was also struggling financially. The loan I took out was all but gone and now we were up to our eyes in debt. I was also becoming more and more disillusioned with what I was witnessing developing within the New Age movement. People were jumping on the bandwagon to 'cash in' on it as it became more 'main stream'. It was also becoming more and more elite, almost to the point of becoming another Religion! Instead of uniting and unifying, it was manifesting more and more separation and a 'holier than thou' type mentality. Some involved were appointing and declaring themselves to be Grand Spiritual Masters - self appointed Gurus with doting devotees. I had had enough! "Where are the genuine folk - ordinary simple good hearted folk?" I thought. I was soon to meet them.

Desperate to earn some money, I took up Painting and Decorating and suddenly I was thrust into the male dominated world of the building site! Talk about a culture shock. I have always maintained great courtesy and respect for the feminine gender, yet here I was surrounded by men, who at the sight of a young lady passing by would shout, whistle and make obscene gestures in her direction. I have never felt so embarrassed. I felt really sorry for the young lady who was subjected to this lewd behaviour. However, underneath this brash, rough and ready facade I discovered individuals with 'hearts of gold'. Most would go out of their way to help anybody that might need it. One such chap named Jacko, took me under his wing and taught me the ropes and we became good friends. I soon became an excellent professional Decorator and kept at it for three years. Finally I could not stand it anymore as my confidence was at an all time low - I needed to get back to my music. So I quit the decorating business!

## Chapter Twelve: Gateways to the Stars!

It was now 1993 and not knowing exactly where I was going next, I decided I wanted to create some 'fun' music. This took the form of a band I created named *Crazy for Animals*. My daughter Anna, who was now 12 years old at this time, had formed her own club that was in aid of protecting animals and wildlife. The name of her club was *Crazy for Animals*! So I wanted to pay tribute to her efforts. We played at the Glastonbury Festival in the 'Green Fields' and we had a lot of fun. Prompted by a casual comment from my dear friend Jon Wadge (who originally got me started as a Psychic Artist), I also started developing the ability to draw peoples personal Spirit Guides. The furthest thing from my mind at the time was that I would ever do this as a profession. I was simply exploring my own potential.

Having spent all those many years as a Portrait Artist, I would always start with a rough shaded sketch (always starting from the eyes out). I would then build up the detail. Whereas I had always had a sitter in front of me to draw from, this was a bit more unusual for there was no visible sitter. So I just allowed the image to take its own form from the rough shaded sketch. I had no idea as to whether I was actually drawing a Spirit Guide or not, so I decided to just simply *trust* that it was. At first I just did it for friends who gave me interesting feedback, though there was nothing conclusive about who I had drawn. Then when I got a little braver, I would carry a sketchpad around with me and whenever the opportune moment arose, I would make a sketch. I even started to do this with casual acquaintances.

Then, on one particular occasion when I was auditioning a female Singer for my new band, I drew her a quick portrait whilst she was out the room making a cup of tea. On her return I showed her the portrait. To my surprise she nonchalantly remarked "Oh! Eagle Hawk - I wonder what he wants"! I asked whether she recognised the Guide, to which she confirmed she did and that she saw him all the time! It turned out that as well as being a Singer she was also a Psychic Reader. This gave me a real boost of confidence.

In between developing this particular gift I was starting to get inspirations for a new album. I wanted this album to have a dance feel and I also wanted to create a brand new band. My interest in Spiritual matters was still expanding and by now I had experienced the opportunity of visiting a number of Crop Circles that were now a regular feature in the crop fields of England every year during the Summer. Some of the shapes were amazing and becoming more and more intricate and complex. These intriguing shapes were turning up in a matter of a few hours! 'What on Earth' was going on - how were they created? Well, first let's look at the TV and media explanation. Suddenly, out of the blue, two gentlemen by the name of Doug and Dave claimed they were responsible for the Crop Circle creations - all done with a piece of string attached to a pole!!! Well this is interesting, as how do they explain the fact that there was no evidence of footmarks? They didn't. How did they explain that some of the crop was bent on the nodes of the wheat (which are extremely brittle)? They didn't. How did they explain that the corn within a Crop Circle had evidence of being chemically changed, almost akin to being micro-waved? They couldn't. How did they explain such complex creations being made in the pitch-black of night without the aid of any lighting and within a couple of hours? Again they didn't!

However, because they were on TV, backed by the media - almost everybody believed them!

What happened when challenged to create some of the more complex patterns? They couldn't - or they would say that they weren't responsible for that particular one! Having personally viewed some of these complex enigmas and taken samples of the corn that were bent at the nodes, there is absolutely no doubt in my mind that Doug and Dave didn't make them. It still leaves the question - who did? Are they extraterrestrial or inter-dimensional consciousnesses? Who knows, except that the appearance of these amazing patterns always occur after sightings of UFO's over the area.

Another alternative explanation could perhaps be Collective Consciousness. There is increasing evidence that the general consciousness is expanding and growing, as more and more individuals develop their own Spiritual understanding. Most Spiritual Wisdom claims that 'thought creates reality', i.e., all that we perceive in our physical world. Is there evidence for this? Well, a number of individuals have been researched regarding their ability of 'mind over matter' - Uri Gellar for instance (although not without controversy), who has been subject to extensive test's under laboratory conditions. He also seems to be able to 'trigger' other people to do the same as him.

I was also very intrigued by some of the new discoveries being made by Quantum Physicists. The generally held view of Scientists prior to this, was that the atom was the smallest particle and was the building block for physical matter. However,

Quantum Physics took us into the realms of the sub-atomic world - discovering particles even smaller! On observing this sub-atomic realm. a particular particle, I believe it is called a 'quark' was observed. On trying to determine the particular function of this enigmatic particle, Physicists were perturbed and surprised to observe that this particle was directly affected by the 'thought' of the observer! Other Scientists and Physicists conducting the same experiments all observed the same phenomena - their minds were directly affecting matter.

Another intriguing concept that has manifest from Quantum Physics is the idea of the 'Holographic Universe'. Up until this point, I had no idea how a 'hologram' was created. A hologram is an image that has the appearance of being three-dimensional and can be viewed from the front and each side (as yet one cannot view the back as far as I know). A hologram is created by taking an object and directing two laser beams at it - the image is then projected onto a special glass, then, when a light is shone upon it you can see the object three dimensionally. What I did not realise is that in the creation of the hologram, it is not a visual image projected onto the glass, instead it is just a 'wave form' - a beam of energy - very interesting!). Now if one was to take the glass plate containing the 3D image and shatter the glass, it would be observed that in each tiny fragment of glass the whole 3D image could still be seen - fascinating!

The idea behind the Holographic Universe is that each tiny particle contains the whole and the whole is contained within it. Does this not sound like the teachings and wisdom that has existed for eons in many Spiritual philosophies? Quantum Physics also acknowledges multi-dimensional realities, in other words many different alternate dimensions or planes of existence. For instance, the realm that we are currently experiencing is referred to as the 3$^{rd}$ Dimension. Beyond this are the 4$^{th}$, 5$^{th}$, 6$^{th}$, 7$^{th}$...ad infinitum and each dimension is determined by its vibrational frequency (the rate or speed of its vibration). This again is interesting, because if one looks at some of the ancient Spiritual wisdoms, this knowledge is again in evidence. Even the Bible speaks of 'Gods house of many mansions'. Spiritualists talk about the numerous 'planes' of existence. Many tribal cultures including Native Americans, Aborigines etc, all accept these other realms as real, and furthermore understand how to access them.

I was at a point in my life where I was reviewing many of the ideas and perspectives that I had previously held and was looking to see if there was a need to re-evaluate them. I started reviewing a number of experiences that were somewhat perturbing to me regarding psychics and mediums that would give messages to me without my consent. Some of the information I was given started to make me feel like I was having no say in what lay before me and I thought "wait a minute, I have my own mind, I can make my own choices"! I wanted to be my own channel.

I suddenly recalled a request or commitment that I had made twenty years earlier - that of being a 'servant of Spirit' I suddenly realised that I no longer wished to be a 'servant'. Without jeopardising any of my principles, I made a new commitment, that of 'Co-creator with Spirit'. After all, in truth everything is Spirit, so why be subservient to it! Co-creation, now what does this imply? Well firstly it requires the acceptance that everything one is to experience in one's own reality, is self-created. Accepting full responsibility for anything that manifests. Phew! No more pointing the finger at others or blaming circumstances. This was a big step!

Okay, so accepting that this is my own choice, what was I to do with it? Well, first I needed to dis-create a few items, like the idea of needing to suffer in order to produce inspiring musical works (like those Composers I had admired in the past). And what about a new creation - to be my own channel? Yes, I liked that one, no more relying on others to channel for me - I wanted to develop my own personal direct link to the Source.

Pondering on all the above insights inspired me further on the development of my next album, which I decided was going to be a double concept album (seeing that I hadn't written anything for a few years now). As I have already mentioned I also wanted the album to have a dance element. After deep pondering I came up with a name for a new band - *Elfin Spiral*. This to me encapsulated the Nature Spirits which links with the Earth, and the spiral links to the inner world and the Stars.

The new double album became entitled *Celestial Gateways and Tribal Awakenings*. *Celestial Gateways* refers to doorways or 'Star Gates' that enable one to enter other dimensions and access multi-dimensional universes and consciousnesses. The idea being that our consciousness exists NOW in many dimensions or realities, perhaps even parallel worlds or other planetary systems simultaneously. It must be possible to access, awaken or 'tune in' to these other realities. This concept would also include the existence of extraterrestrial life forms (what I call Star-Beings or Star-People). There has been a tremendous amount of evidence available to support these ideas.

*Tribal Awakenings* is about exploring and tapping into one's own ancient ancestry, which also explores genetic memory. I had been exploring the concept that each tiny minute cell that evolved into our current physical bodies has it's own consciousness and therefore it's own memory. I had a profound experience out in Nature in the woods one day, when I had a startling insight! We as humans, are like the hologram, though we are singular units - like a single cell. We also contain the whole and the whole is contained within us. In reality there is no separation - this is merely an illusion. It is interesting to note that every element found in Nature is contained within our bodies. The inference of this has further connotations, because if one chooses to accept this idea then nothing can ever be alien to us! How can anything really harm us if it is contained within us? This required much thought and assimilation, however I felt a resonance with the whole concept, as it made a lot of sense in light of what I was experiencing. It was one of those curious 'inner knowings'.

The first track I wrote for the new album was entitled *The Vortex*. This was followed by other tracks including *Star-Gate* and *Dreamland 5*. I had been working on the album for about two months when a friend who owned a New Age shop, asked me if I would be interested in reviewing a manuscript of a new book that was soon to be published. The book was written by an amateur Quantum Physicist named David Ash, who also embraced Spiritual understandings. The book highlighted the insights that Quantum Physics was uncovering that paralleled many of the ancient Spiritual wisdoms. The title of the book was *The Vortex (The Science of Ascension)*. This blew me away - yet another synchronicity. Then there was more…

A close friend turned up one day clutching a New Age publication that had an article he thought I would be interested in. The article was all about Star Gates! A group of individuals had devised a geometric structure that contained many pyramidal shapes and was made of copper filled with a saline solution. The idea for this structure was that if one was to sit within it, one could experience $5^{th}$ Dimensional consciousness! I had read many scientific reports about the energies that pyramids harness, although it was not fully understood. It was confirmed that somehow this shape did manifest an energy. I remember years earlier I had played about with an open frame pyramid that was a scaled down version of the dimensions and angles of the great pyramid of Giza, where incidentally it had been discovered that certain foods and wheat had been perfectly preserved for centuries! The experiments I conducted confirmed that indeed food such as bread or apples, that were stored under the pyramid, stayed fresher than those outside. Another interesting experiment I did was with honey placed in a saucer! The honey changed it's consistency depending on the alignment of the pyramid. Turned one way the honey turned to liquid, turned another it crystallized! More enigmas to ponder!

But back to the album, and yet another curious synchronicity. I received a call from a Psychic friend who would often call me to relate curious messages that she thought I would understand. On this particular occasion she started querying me as to what "Dreamland 5" was? I replied that I had no idea. She then went on to say that the only thing that she could see (in her mind's eye) was a domed structure somewhere out in the desert and that when one entered and descended down some steps, there was a room full of computers. After her call I thought about this one! I had heard stories and rumours of secret bases housing crashed UFO's and experiments with alien technology - was this one such place? The whole idea of this inspired the track *Dreamland 5* and I felt inspired to write a few lines of lyrics to accompany it, which went as follows:-
*Time for the secrets to be told*
*Time that the mysteries unfold*
*Dreams of the dreamers come to be*
*All that was hidden is now open to you - open to me - reality changes when you are free*

Imagine how startled I was when another friend came to see me and handed me another New Age magazine that contained an article written by an ex-Navel Intelligence Officer reporting on a secret base in the Nevada Desert, USA. The code name for this base was 'DREAMLAND' also known as 'Area 51'! According to the article, Scientists were 'back engineering' and experimenting with extraterrestrial technologies and spacecraft at this highly guarded secretive base...I was once again amazed at the synchronicity.

During the period I was writing this album, a group of friends decided it would be fun to set up a UFO Group. It was now 1994. One particular friend had come across some interesting videos which had footage showing UFO's across the world, and contained interviews with individuals who had experienced actual encounters. I did not realise how much information was out there. The group attracted many interesting people, one in particular had been extensively studying the Crop Circle phenomena and he showed us a video taken by a young lad who had decided to stay up all night, armed with his video camera. He camped in an area that was prolific for Crop Circle manifestations and furthermore had been the location of sightings of many strange lights that had been witnessed at regular intervals. The video contained footage of an open field with two lights shooting into view, whilst circling the fields. One could witness the crop below suddenly flatten down into a complex pattern. This footage has since become an extremely controversial piece of film -unsurprisingly!

As the UFO Group got bigger and bigger we decided to hold a public event, enabling the general public to view the videos and information that we were discovering. We decided to call this event *First Contact* and it was extremely successful. We concluded the evening with a music concert featuring my *Elfin Spiral* band, performing the new album. Literally, that same week that we decided to share our knowledge and discoveries to the general public, a new series was launched on national TV - *The X-Files* - with its catch phrase being "The truth is out there".

Another amazing synchronicity  or was it that we were we actually creating the reality?!!!

## Chapter Thirteen: My First Contact

By 1994/5 I was still working on the 2nd half of the album (*Tribal Awakenings*) whilst continuing to develop my Psychic portraits. An opportunity arose out of the blue when I met a Medium in a local New Age shop whilst trying to promote my other albums and inspirational cards that I had produced from my original artwork. We got into interesting conversation and I happened to mention that I was developing the ability to draw people's Spirit Guides and she got very excited. She had been looking for a Psychic Artist to draw three of her own Guides. She immediately commissioned me to draw them saying that she would pay me! Up until this point I had not considered doing this as a paid profession. However she insisted and before I knew it I was suddenly in demand. Outlets for my gift literally manifested out of thin air. I was very nervous about actually charging a fee for the portraits, particularly as I had no idea who I was drawing and was not able to give any information. However the Medium that had been my first paying customer, reassured me and told me not to worry about it, as information would come eventually. She encouraged me to continue, she even went so far as to recommend me to work in a local New Age shop run by a friend of hers in Dorking.

In no time at all, word had got around and I was in much demand. Another New Age shop - *The Golden Bough* in Croydon - invited me to a days session with them and said they would ensure that I would have customers already lined up. They asked me whether I minded if they got the local newspaper to come in and conduct an interview, giving both the shop and myself some publicity and exposure. This in itself became another curious synchronicity. I had drawn a number of portraits on this occasion, which weren't immediately recognised by the sitter. Then my next sitter arrived and I started to draw the portrait. She was with a friend and I couldn't help over hearing her conversation. It seemed she was hoping for a Native American Guide that she was already aware of. I looked at the image I was drawing - not a Native American at all - instead it was of a young man. I started to feel a bit nervous, thinking that she was going to be disappointed. However I continued with the picture, allowing it to be whatever was manifesting on the paper. I finished the portrait and just as I presented it to her the Journalist from the local newspaper walked in and was witness to my client suddenly bursting into tears exclaiming "You've drawn my son"! (One of her son's had sadly died recently). The

Journalist couldn't have timed his arrival better (or yet another synchronicity?!). This was "a great story" he excitedly remarked!

The next day there I was in the local papers - *Putting Psychic Power on Show - Psychic Artist Brings Forth Mrs Butler's Son!* it read. Unbeknown to me, the circulation of the local paper spread further than I realised and the editor of *Psychic News* (an established newspaper and journal that has been going since the 1930's) spied my article. Next thing I knew I was invited for an interview which went out as a feature in their very next publication! I was on the map. This exposure generated a wealth of interest and commissions. Everything was happening so fast!

I felt a need to understand the process that was enabling me to produce Spirit Guides, particularly in light of having no idea who I was drawing. After much pondering and deliberation this is what was revealed to me…

The very first step I made, was to make an INTENTION, which was to simply ask if I could channel through the Spirit guides. I decided to do it within a framework of providing a 'tool' that the individual could work with themselves and would further empower and assist them to communicate directly with their Guides, thus enabling them to become their own channel. What did I do next? Well, after trying to figure out or try and tune in as to whom I was drawing (which caused me a great deal of trials and tribulations), I decided to simply TRUST that whatever manifested was totally appropriate for the individual I was drawing the portrait for. This initially was not so easy however I persevered.
There is a third element to this process, probably the most important of all. Although I was trusting the process whilst drawing, I still found myself trying to figure out who I was tuning into - again this caused me a great deal of perplexing. I finally decided not to try and figure it out at all, but just to simply ALLOW it to be whatever it was to be. This is probably the most crucial and important aspect of this simple 3-step process:-

1)       INTENTION
2)       TRUST
3)       ALLOWANCE

The allowance was the key, in that it entailed the removal of any preconceived ideas, expectations or attachment to the outcome. I just had to totally remove myself and draw the picture. So this was the formulae I used for the manifestation of Spiritual Guides. This process was completely in accord with the concept of co-creating with Spirit. I decided it to be - and so it was!!!

It didn't immediately hit me straight away as to the significance and potential of what I had first discovered, but it eventually dawned on me that if this 3-step process for manifestation works in this instance (and I have a wealth of evidence that it did, including personal testimonies from sitters and recognition from a number of established reputable Psychic and Spiritual establishments and development centres), there is no reason why it could not be used for manifestation in any other area of endeavour. I was startled by the potency of such a discovery - the next step was to put it to the test!

This is what I discovered...

When I applied this process to things that I did not have a particularly strong attachment to or any preconceived expectation, then the process worked perfectly - in fact many individuals have inadvertently used this process without even knowing it. For example, how many times has a situation like this occurred; your iron breaks down or your vacuum cleaner and you've have the briefest thought "Oh damn I need to replace it". Then within a few moments something else distracts you and you forget all about it and then in some cases, after a few hours or a day or two, somebody mentions that "so and so" has an iron or vacuum cleaner they want to get rid of, and do you know anyone who wants one? This has happened to me on countless occasions.

To continue with experimenting with the process, when I have applied it to things that I have a strong attachment to or expectation - even with the purest of intentions, then invariably I have been disappointed. Why is this? Perhaps it has to do with the nature of attachment or expectation. To some degree, there is an element of either desperation or doubt, both of which are based on fear, for example the fear that it may not happen or you won't get it. Sometimes it could even be the fear that you *will* get it and it might change you! I have encountered many individuals who are afraid of success rather than failure. I know I have experienced this myself. What is happening here, is that although one has made their intention and then trusted the process, there has been no allowance because fear is now added to the original intention. So one may get or achieve whatever they made their intention for, but it will either manifest or come about in a fearful way. Or you could also view it, that once fear or doubt has entered the picture there is no longer any trust. The positive aspect of my own discoveries, was that it enabled me to see where I was still conditioned in certain areas of my life and where I still had deep attachment or expectations. This was of immense personal value, because I could now work on harmonising them and bring them into balance. Replacing fear with love or perhaps learning to love one's fears? That's a bizarre thought, offering love to the fear!

Learning to love one-self is certainly becoming a common theme, or choosing to make love the basis of one's life existence. If we go back to the Holographic Universe concept, that though we are fragments we each contain the whole, the 'all that is', then we must also surely effect it - so choosing love as the hub of the wheel so to speak, is surely an idea worth exploring and living.

This was the point that I was at - endeavouring to be a living example of love in action, integrating light and shadow, seeking a different expression that operates beyond the dualities. A lot of information was coming forth regarding a major shift in consciousness occurring within mankind, brought about by an acceleration in the vibrational frequency of the Earth and moving us into a higher dimension (some suggest the 5$^{th}$ dimension). This is also having a dramatic effect on our concept of 'time'. More and more individuals I meet, myself included, are focusing more on living in the NOW, rather than focusing either too much on the past or too much on the future - for both have the potential of robbing one from the PRESENT - the gift in the NOW. I also found it interesting to observe, that the same mental facilities are used when remembering the past as are used for visualising the future. Both employ the imagination (or thoughts in our head), the only difference is that we conceive the past to be real and the future imagined. I found myself pondering more and more on the significance of all this. Is this what some of the Prophecies have been referring to? For example the Hopi Indians and the Mayans (and their Mayan Calendar) speak of the 'End Times' occurring around the year 2012/13. Many people interpret this as the end of the world. Perhaps it simply means the end of 'time' as we know it? Many folk I've met have commented on feeling like time is speeding up - suppose it is not speeding up as such, but merely becoming shorter.

These concepts were occupying a great deal of my time and the implications were fascinating.  If we go back again to the discovery in Quantum Physics - of the enigmatic little particle called the 'quark' that responded to the thoughts of the observer and did whatever the observer thought it would - this then ties in completely with the 3-step process I had discovered, and made perfect sense as to why it works. To explain; when one makes an *intention*, instructions are sent to this tiny quark that sets about manifesting the desired thought. By *trusting*, it enables it to go about its business unheeded by any further counter instructions like worrying for instance, because one has then added doubt - or even over-planning or trying to figure out how it will manifest - because then one is limiting the manifestation - rather like saying "I want this, but it has to happen this way or that way". Over-worrying or over-planning is *not* allowing. Left to its own devices the little quark will find the quickest and easiest way to manifest. Now remembering that the quark is a particle smaller than an atom and exists in the sub atomic realms (or dimensions), it has got to work its way through many layers before manifesting in the physical or 3D realm - in other words it takes a period of time. Therefore one could view time as simply being the delay between thinking a thought and it's physical manifestation. This is interesting because it has been frequently stated from many sources, that for those that exist in the Spiritual realms, time does not exist. There is only NOW - to them, past, present and future all exist in the same space and are simply different dimensions of the NOW. This idea incidentally, is also being expressed and understood in Quantum Physics!

So going back to the idea of 'time shortening' - as the vibrational frequency of the 3$^{rd}$ Dimension increases, so the delay between thought and manifestation is not taking as long! This has immense connotations and implications. One that immediately struck me was the need to monitor our thoughts, because left unchecked, we could well be manifesting all manner of undesirable outcomes. I decided to spend a whole day monitoring my thoughts and every time I found myself entertaining dis-empowering thoughts, I would consciously change it to an empowering one. In this way I was re-programming myself, for I was well aware that I could have a mass of stored conditioned processes lurking in my sub-consciousness. This was going to take some dedicated effort!

By the year 1997, I had completed the *Celestial Gateways/Tribal Awakenings* album and had performed it at numerous outdoor festivals, including the major Glastonbury Festival, with my band *Elfin Spiral*, and we were enthusiastically received.

I had now also become well established as a Psychic Artist and my reputation was growing to the extent that I was frequently asked to demonstrate my gift at a variety of Spiritual and Psychic development centres, including the *S.A.G.B (Spiritualist Association of Great Britain)* in Belgrave Square, London - an establishment founded in the 1930's by Sir Arthur Conan Doyle. I felt very honoured.

Intriguing developments were starting to take place regarding the Guides I was now bringing through. When I first started channelling Guides, I thought that I was going to get aunties, uncles, grandparents and other relatives, or maybe some ancient ancestors like Native Americans or Chinese Guides and I certainly did (and still do) get quite a few of these. However it soon became apparent that I was starting to bring through a lot of Star- Beings (some may call them extraterrestrials).

The very first time this occurred, I had already started to pick up some information about the Guides I was drawing. On this particular occasion, I was linking in for a client - an elderly gentleman who just seemed a normal ordinary genuinely pleasant individual. He showed no evidence of being either 'way out' or 'wacky'! On completion of his Spirit Guide I was immediately struck with the thought that who I had drawn was a Star-Being! "Oh", I thought "how do I tell him - should I even mention it"? I initially skirted around the subject staying more with the general account of why the Guide had come to him and how it could help. Then, right at the end I asked him what he felt about 'beings' existing on other planets. His response was immediate - "Oh", he said, "I certainly do believe they exist, as I get one talking to me all the time"! He went on to explain that he had received telepathic messages from a Star-Being during meditations - although he had never seen them. He was highly delighted when I told him that his Guide whom I had drawn was from the Stars!

This situation became increasingly common, particularly the response from my clients
- they had absolutely no qualms at all about accepting life on other planets. I was meeting people from all walks of life who were quite happy to accept a different reality to the considered norm!

I remember another surprising incident along the same lines. You may recall that my initial introduction to Mediums, Psychics and Healers came about from my Mum inviting me to a talk at a Spiritualist Church, through which I discovered a lot with which I felt a resonance with. I never felt however, inclined to label myself a 'Spiritualist' as I am not one for being labelled or put into a category - I prefer to be a *free Spirit*! The main focus of the

Spiritualist association was to prove survival after death and concentrated on bringing through evidence of departed relatives and family. However, on this one occasion I was invited to demonstrate my gift at a Spiritualist Church in Guildford.

Generally, when I do a demonstration, I work in conjunction with one of their own resident Mediums even though I may have never met them before. On arrival, I was greeted warmly and introduced to the Medium I was to work with. I usually commence with a very quick drawing of a Guide and then the Medium locates the individual that the picture is intended for (from the audience) and then channels the message from the Guide to them.

To my utter amazement nearly all the pictures I drew that evening were Star-Beings! At the end of the evening I spoke to the lady that ran the centre and asked what was going on! I did not think the Spiritualist Church was 'in' to 'Star-Beings', to which she laughingly replied that their center was an unusual one and that they were attempting to expand the narrow parameters that are usually laid down. What was even more surprising, was when she told me that the lady that was working with me that night as the Medium, was in a state of utter astonishment, as up until that night she had not believed in Star-Beings and yet there she was channelling them!

1997 rolled into 1998 and I continued working professionally as a Psychic Artist and still predominantly found myself drawing Star-Beings. At the same time I was coming across books and literature - mostly channelled information of communications from a wide range of different Star-Being Groups. The information contained therein was practically identical to the understandings that I had intuitively been exposed to, which to me was a confirmation of my own inner channelling. I was now recognising that I had always been my own channel. The synchronicities that had occurred each time I came up with a theme for my music further confirmed this. As I reviewed the concepts for each of the albums, I realised that I subsequently lived and manifested these themes in my physical reality. A prime example of this, being the period during the creation of the album *Out of the Mist (The Quest for Avalon)*. There was much for me to absorb and still many, many more questions. So, do I really create my own reality? Well, I certainly create the way I choose to experience it. But, what actually is reality? Reality is often expressed as something that one has had a personal experience of.

Many individuals have claimed to have had a vast array of experiences, some of which do not fall into the category of the accepted norm (whatever that is)! They have had experiences that perhaps defied the known logic of accepted facts, be they Scientific or even Spiritual. But, if we consider that the parameters of the above are surely only what is currently understood at the time, i.e., the best possible understanding in the light of the evidence available, or even what can be mutually agreed upon, this also raises interesting questions because perhaps what one regards as 'normal', is determined by 'Mass Consensus'. An interesting book I read went further in to this topic and described it as 'Morphogenic Resonance', which is the general reality we all experience created by mutual agreement by the masses. This does not mean that it is the only reality! There are many individuals that are defying the accepted norm all the time. Surely there is no end to the limitless possibilities we can create, is there? We only have to look at our history to discover that things we would once have thought impossible are now commonplace in our everyday lives including; modern telephones, computers, lasers, ships to the moon, digital special effects and virtual reality, to name but a few. This leads me to believe that if we can imagine it, we can surely create it.

Imagination and creativity are the tools for manifestation. My own experiences certainly confirm this. On the other hand - do we create our reality, or is it that reality just *is*, and we are being imaginative in the way we choose to experience it? What of Illusion then? It is often described as something that isn't real, a 'no-thing', yet, at some time or other we have had experiences of it! It can all get quite confusing can it not?!

It was whilst pondering all the above thoughts, that it struck me how interesting the bias we place on certain words used in the English Language. For example, the word *dis-illusion* is generally used to describe an undesirable state to be in. Yet, surely what the word actually means is to *dissolve illusion* - which is surely a beneficial state? How curious that many of the commonly understood meanings of some words have been overlaid with a distortion. There are many other interesting examples.

*Responsibility* is often depicted as some kind of burden thrust upon us by an authorative figure like a teacher or a parent. We are told to "Face up to your responsibilities", yet, if one actually looks at the word *response ability* it simply means the ability to respond.

The word *self-centered* is generally used in the same context as selfish. Yet most Spiritual disciplines encourage one to be 'centred' within the Self.

*Beware* - often used in a scary or fearful context - simply means *be aware*.

*Induce* is yet another interesting word, with its companion *Induction*. To induce someone to do something has the implications of heavy persuading (almost forcing, like 'inducing labour'). It is interesting that many businesses now run 'induction courses'!

These are just a few examples of the many words that when looked at, often have a completely different meaning to the context in which they are generally used.

So where do we go from here! If we really do create our own reality, what reality do we want to create? Perhaps we could create the 'joy of being', instead of continually being caught up in 'doing'. A Human - *Being*, instead of a Human - *Doing*! Perhaps we could create a means of moving out of the continual duality game of the 'them and us' scenarios and the "I am right you are wrong' game.

What of all the other dis-empowering syndromes like; "Do as you are told", "Stay in your place", "I am in control", "Don't question me", "You owe me"... and so on.

During the period mentioned earlier, regarding the monitoring of one's thoughts, I also came across a wealth of common expressions that everyone uses daily, all of which have a dis-empowering bias.

For example, the word and expression *"Typical"* is often used in a negative way. You may think or exclaim it when you are about to park your car in a parking space, but someone else beats you to it! Or when it has been sunny all week whilst you have been indoors working, but on your day off it rains! If you were to examine what you are actually saying to yourself - you are saying it's typical that someone always gets there before you, or that your day off is bound to be spoilt. It therefore has a victim consciousness behind it, like something is deliberately trying to thwart you - this is not an empowering thought.

Then there's the expression *"That's life"* (I really dislike this one!). It has such a loaded feeling of despair and hopelessness, it is like saying that we don't have any choice or we can't change anything.

What about when someone offers to do us a favour or give us a gift or help? You may say "Oh, you shouldn't have" or "Don't worry about me - I'll be alright" - all being indicative of an inability to receive. I have been amazed at the number of wonderful individuals I have met that are extremely generous with their giving, but are incredibly reticent and awkward about receiving (I have been guilty of this too)! Often this is indicative of a low self-esteem and lack of self-worth and value.

As for me, I choose to create an empowering way of life with *love* as it's basis. This requires loving one-self unconditionally (a challenge for us all!). This choice also entails becoming the 'answer' to one's own questions.

During the Christmas period I had a powerful insight. I knew that a 'new energy' was permeating our current existence. At first I tried to figure it out - then I decided to 'hold on', thinking that if I just allowed it to unfold, that the understanding would reveal itself. Thus, I *chose* to be the *'light of my own Star'*!

Then I really was put to the test!...

## Chapter Fourteen: The End?

I thought this book was complete - yet four years has passed since last writing and it has been the most extraordinary four years - a period whereby I was to have to pull out all the stops, so to speak, and really 'walk the talk' and embrace all the insights and their true meanings.

To talk about being challenged on all levels would be an understatement. I can recall a 'request' I made whilst coming to the understanding that our reality is 'coloured' by our 'beliefs' and I wondered what my reality would be like if I removed all my currently held beliefs. But once again be careful what you ask for you might just get it!

Shortly after completing (or so I thought) this book, my relationship with my partner of fifteen years took a turn for the worst and she left me for someone else. To be fair we had been under considerable strain for a number of years, due mainly to financial pressure and my eternal optimism only seemed to aggravate the situation as far as my partner was concerned. Suffice to say that we had already become estranged and so I understand her need to explore a 'new' dimension that would hopefully bring her the fulfilment that she felt she required.

I have to admit that I took it really badly at first, but I eventually managed to let her go with love. For the first month or so, I was actually surprised at how well I coped and just focused on attempting to maintain the payments of our jointly owned flat whilst preparing for it's sale. What actually occurred a few months down the line - I was not prepared for...

The flat took a whole year to sell, which, without going into detail, had been an extremely unpleasant and dis-empowering time involving legal matters. Two weeks before I had to vacate the flat which had now been sold, I awoke one morning with panic attacks! These lasted every single moment of every single day for the next eight months! At the same time, the one person that had been one of my greatest supports - my Mother (the only member of my family that truly understood me) - suffered a mild stroke and developed dementure. In fact everything that gave me comfort and safety was gradually stripped away from me - even my *sense of Spirit*. Places in Nature that had held wonderful memories of upliftment and inner peace - filled me with terror! You could truly say I went into the 'Void' - nothing meant anything to me anymore and all I felt was FEAR, grief and terror. I became afraid of everything. I could not be on my own and it was only through the support of my children and dear friends that I got through each day.

During this time I met a wonderful supportive lady who became my friend and counsel - she was a Wiccan High Priestess - and I became afraid of her, such was my loss of all rationality. This in itself was a strange paradox, as I had become reliant on her for emotional support and at the same point during this dark, dark time, I wanted to escape her! There were points during this dark phase, where I thought I was going to go insane - nothing seemed to make me feel better. I had received healing of all kinds. Somehow through all this, I still managed to work. My main source of income was drawing Spirit Guides, either by post or at holistic Spiritual fayres and exhibitions.

You can probably imagine the soul searching I went through at this time. How could I be bringing through some sort of guidance for others, when I was in such a state! I truly honestly didn't even know whether I was channeling any more or whether I really was just making it all up!!!

I came to realise that the only way to break through this unnamed fear (because I did not truly know what it was I was fearing - it had all become too muddled) was to face *a fear*, any fear, in other words, *do something* - anything that took courage. I thought that maybe doing something like a parachute jump might be a start. Facing *a physical* fear. However, after considering the cost I realised that for the same amount of money, I could take a trip to America, as I had been in receipt of an invitation by a friend whom had kept in touch with me from the visit I had made there ten years earlier. I had only met him the one time when he had offered his hospitality in his home for a week to my previous partner and myself. In my current state though, the thought of travelling across the world on my own, leaving my family and friends (of whom I had come to *need* for support) to meet up with someone I didn't really know and furthermore was also a practicing Wiccan, filled me with even more dread and terror!

Eight months had gone by and I was at my wit's end - *I had to do something* or I felt I was doomed. I thought that I could at least enquire about possible flights to the USA and on making enquiries, I suddenly found myself booking the flight! I did this just before Christmas 1998 and I booked to go the day before New Years Eve! It is hard to explain to anyone, unless they have experienced a similar predicament, just how dysfunctional I felt. Things that I wouldn't even think twice about, took incredible effort to comprehend let alone do. So you can imagine how I felt as I stepped out onto the plane. All I could do was to stay in each moment as it arose - as soon as I thought too far ahead - I felt panic.

Once in the air I thought "My God - I'm doing it - I am on my *own* heading across the world"! I must have spent most of that journey just staring out the window, allowing myself to get lost in the amazing cloud formations. This became the turning point for me, I had reached *inside* and found some *courage*. I had faced fear and looked it in the eye.

I ended up spending a month, instead of my previously booked two weeks, in the States, during which time I just soaked in the Sun and spent my time in meditation - bringing the golden sun rays into my being. The rest of the time was spent relearning some of my earlier music from *The River Song Suite* album, which I had composed on my acoustic guitar. Gradually I found myself coming back to *my self*. I also realised that there was a whole new life awaiting for me to explore. By the time my month was over and I returned to England, I was filled with a renewed Vision. No longer was I afraid to be on my own. I had a new goal now to aspire to.

I had originally intended to return to the States in the Spring and I only came back to the UK to tie up loose ends and prepare myself for my new life. It was such a joy to get in my car on my return and catch up with my children and friends, driving here, there and everywhere.

A few days after my return, I attended a small holistic fayre and received a wonderful channelling from a lady named Ann, who has since become a close and dear friend. She confirmed that my Spiritual Pathway was to be fulfilled in the States. As Spring grew closer I decided to delay my return a few more months so as to build up some financial resources by attending the many fayres that ran through until June. I booked my flight in advance and was eagerly preparing for this new dimension to my life. Then a lady came into my life - a dear soul and my heart went out to her. My compassion for her overwhelmed me and I made one of the biggest mistakes ever - I thought I could rescue her.

This was to have disastrous results on me and my well-being, although now in hindsight, I realise it was a gift in disguise...but more of that later. I was still very vulnerable myself and two weeks before I was to depart to the States - I 'wobbled' and I did not go. Instead I found myself moving in with my new lady friend.

I do not wish to give a detailed account of this relationship, except that she had a major addiction to alcohol (which she denied), and which I thought I could help her overcome. This nearly destroyed me. I found myself having panic attacks again. Four times we split up, until finally I could not bear the emotional pain anymore and had to leave. I felt that the wound of losing a loved one and a home, was being re-enacted over and over again. I had no idea what I was to do next - I couldn't even think about it.

I decided to visit some dear friends that ran a healing centre called *Rivendell* - that was also their home. It was a beautiful farmhouse set in the countryside near Essex. These wonderful friends offered me a room to use as a sanctuary, and so began my real healing. I was to stay there for eight months, during which time resulted in the most amazing and profound period of insights and recognitions. This was also the first time I was able to set up my music equipment since I lost my own home and started writing a new album (three years had gone by since my last album). I entitled this new album (which I channeled through a being called RAEL) *With Eyes Wide Open* and as before with my previous albums, the synchronicities with my life and the concepts of the album soon started to occur again. The first recognition I made, was that of taking responsibility for the reality I had created. So I had to honestly ask myself why I had attracted all the situations or people into my life. The most profound recognition I made, was that everything that had happened to me really was a gift, regardless of the packaging it was wrapped up in. The four times I split up with the dear lady friend with the addiction resulted in her literally 'throwing' me out the house, and I realised that she was actually *giving me back to myself.* I had become 'lost' in her and her problems, I had let slide so much of myself. With this recognition, I could only bless and thank her for this gift. All feelings of pain, hurt or anger dissolved and all I felt for her was compassionate love.
I had been reminded of the profound experience in the woods that I had had years earlier, whereby I had been made aware that all that I perceive as external to me, is who *I am*, and that which I think of as me (in this physical embodiment) is merely a monitor to experience *my self*. I now decided to take this concept a stage further and discover the full potential of this insight. This meant I had to find new ways to gage my interactions with others. I also had to acknowledge that for me to attract someone with an addiction, meant that somewhere I had an addiction. After considerable contemplation and complete honesty, I

realised that I was addicted to the *'need'* for a partner - someone to *'live'* my life for or through, such were the kind of insights that poured forth from my newly found consciousness.

As my new album proceeded, so more and more 'remembrances' came back to me - I felt like *me* again. Bit by bit more things of *true* value returned to me. Another of the profound insights I had regarding my relationship with this 'angel' with the addiction, was that by thinking I could 'rescue' her, I had immediately dis-empowered her and myself. In other words, I was not recognising her own power to change her life - if she really wanted to. We all *choose* the reality we wish to experience (either consciously or unconsciously) and it is not our place to interfere with the free will of other's choices - we can assist if asked and provide tools that will empower them - but it has to be their *own choice* as to whether they use them.

Continuing with the album also assisted me to get through the sadness I felt. During this time I was also exploring in further depth, the concept of multi-dimensionality - which is directly connected to the concept that all time exists in the NOW. Although this concept had inspired me greatly years earlier, I now wanted to explore this much further and make it a living reality.

In between writing the album, I had brought a box full of my old audio cassettes out of storage that contained loads of musical compositions, some of which were in very rough form that went back to the very early beginnings of my musical career. I was now in preparation for my trip to the States again and I thought I would compile various tracks that could perhaps be reworked and updated. I was to suddenly find myself on a musical journey of my life. I remembered having a deep conversation with a good friend of mine on the subject of multi-dimensionality and that all time exists NOW, and how that which we call the past exists NOW and that which we call the future exists NOW. I commented on how interesting it was that when we say that we 'remember' the past and that we' imagine' the future - both are actually using the same mechanism - they are both 'thoughts' in our head. When we are in the NOW this is the only time where we are fully conscious of our present surroundings - anything else is just 'thoughts' in our head. Jokingly I told my friend that I was going to have fun and play with the idea of reversing the concept of past and future. Instead of thinking I remember the past, I was going to decide that I imagined the past, and instead of thinking I imagine the future, I decided I was going to remember the future - in other words - live the future backwards.

What occurred shortly after this - 'blew me away'.

As I continued going through my music tapes, it struck me that the further back I went into the early music, the more 'current' were the themes. The same was true of my more recent compositions, for they reflected ancient times (like the legend of King Arthur and Avalon). I commented on this to my friend and again jokingly remarked that if I carried on like this I would find the next song I was to write!

I continued reviewing my old material on cassette and suddenly came across a piece of music going backwards. I realised that it was a song that I had recorded on an old Four Track Tape Recorder I used to have, which uses ordinary cassettes and enables one to record on all four tracks going in the same direction. The principle of stereo recordings is that it utilises two tracks which can be played on one side (creating the stereo effect) and two tracks on the other side. If you were to play one side of a cassette that had been recorded on the Four Track on a regular cassette player, you would get one side playing two tracks backwards. I was enthralled by the sound of this track going backwards and it immediately inspired me to lay it down on my Eight Track Digital Recorder and build a new song around it. It was only after I had finished it, that I remembered the comment I made to my friend, that if I carried on like this I would find the next track I was going to write…and I had just found it! The further irony of it was, that it was a track going backwards!

Now I was really fired up and excited. I also realised that the multi-dimensional concept that I was 'playing' with, was only part of the story. For what I had done was reverse the concept of linear time, which we think of as an imaginary line that passes from the past into the present and onto the future, and all I did was reverse it. In reality (or multi-dimensional reality) we are in the centre, like the hub of a wheel, with infinite lines (or spokes) that go off in all directions. The implications of this made me realise that everything that ever was or can be, in *all* it's infinite variations - already exists NOW. What we call the past is just another dimension of NOW. What we call the future is just another dimension of NOW. The moment we imagine something, it is already in existence in some dimension. This lent itself to the question of how we bring these other dimensions into our current (present) NOW time. Once again, I thought I would just 'play' with the concept.

I was just at the point of completing the new album *With Eyes*

*Wide Open* when my friends announced they had to sell their farm (the Healing Centre). I was already preparing and saving money for my forthcoming journey to the States. I finally finished the album in March 2001 and had booked my ticket for the following June. I started to wonder what would have happened had I have gone to the States when I had originally intended to two years earlier, before I got sidetracked.

If I applied my new understanding of the multi-dimensional universe, whereby all realities exist in the NOW including 'alternative' realities that exist from 'different' choices we make, then this would imply that when I decided not to take that earlier trip to the USA, another aspect of me in an alternate reality would have made that trip and would already be over there. I pondered what the *'me'* in that reality would have to tell *'me'* about my forthcoming trip! So I decided to ask "What would that *'me'* say to this *'me'* NOW?". I immediately got the impression of a thought that replied "Just be relaxed - go with the flow - I have already made contacts here so you will remember them when you get out here". This was really exciting and guess what - that's exactly what happened!!!

Believe it or not, **we *do* create our own reality** based on what **we *choose*** to embrace. For myself I had already decided to embrace the idea that 'anything is possible' in my reality. I was also to discover some other insights regarding the reality we create, this being that it is a *direct mirror* and reflection of the *view we hold of our self* (both consciously and sub-consciously). The implications of this are immense - for it is important to remember that we have to take into account the sub-conscious view we hold, which is largely coloured by all our conditioning. Furthermore, we are also subject to the genetic memory in our cellular DNA codes. Then of course there is the Mass Consciousness view imposed by the media and society.
The moment we enter a physical body at birth, before we even live this particular life time, we are immediately exposed to the genetic memory of the human race, which includes all its disempowerment, all its suffering and all its fear based conditioning - no wonder we have a tough time being human!
I believe that we are 'Light Workers' and that our job is to 'change' the story - which we do by changing our self, and we do that by changing the *view* of our self. As simple as it sounds, there is logic to it. Consider this, when I was younger and pondered what the 'truth' of things in life were, I had a profound insight. In order to 'know' truth I had to practice truth. By being as truthful and honest as I could be, this would create the energy

and resonance of truth, therefore I would recognise it whenever it was presented as a 'resonance that rung true'. It therefore follows, that by becoming an expression of joy, love and abundance, it would also create a resonance of these energies that would magnetise this into one's existence. Instead of looking for these things externally - I would create it from myself - simply by deciding it *to be*! If I don't like any aspects of myself, then these aspects would manifest in my reality as something that would mirror them...a daunting concept! Therefore the development of discovering things that one could like about one-self, would surely be preferable.

Sometimes some of the most profound Spiritual truths are so very simple, but because we have become so conditioned by complexity, we often miss the point. This brings us back to the earlier insight I was given of; Intention, Trust and Allowance - simple in it's concept, though it requires practice and perseverance to achieve - but is well, well worth it!

It is *my view* in *my reality*, that we are *all* manifestations and *aspects* of the Divine - and to truly honour, value and recognise the Divine, we must honour, value and recognise the Divine that is *our self*. By *allowing* these thoughts of our self, we can eliminate the old conditions of destructive fear based notions of our self. We can liberate ourselves and take humanity onto a completely new level of potentiality. This I feel is our destiny and there is a lot of evidence to support this. We can *choose* to be in synch or not with the universal Divine flow. We can *choose* to operate from FEAR or LOVE. Only we decide. When you are in synch you recognise the synchronicity in your life, and this can be a gage to equate you are on your life path.

Every time I have an experience that causes me to explore new ways of perceiving and result in gaining insights and profound recognitions, either a book or information from some other source comes along that supports exactly the thoughts or ideas that I have embraced. I have listed a number of such source books at the end of this book for further recommended reading.

So this is my story to date and here is a summary of what I perceive of the reality and potential that awaits us all *if we so choose*:-

We are *all* unlimited potential CREATOR GODS AND GODDESSES and our only limitations are those we impose on our self or the way we view our self. We are all 'one' with the universe and multi-universes and beyond consciousnesses, and we exist in infinite forms of creation in all dimensions on all worlds. Nothing is alien to us - for we are all contained within the whole (the 'all that is') and the whole is contained within us - nothing is separate from us.

We are in a process of activation of our cellular genetic codes - this has been discovered and confirmed by Genetic Scientists. This is also activating our 'Star-Seed Genetic Memory' DNA coding inherited from our Ancient Ancestors from the Stars - the Star-Beings/Star-People. This directly relates to the information put forth in the Hopi Indian Prophesies and the Mayan Calendar. The Mayans created a template for the 'new human being' and left a calendar that describes major planetary alignments and conjunctions that serve as triggers (activators) to our genetic coding, which will enable us to access our true multi-dimensional awareness, which will in turn cause us to 'remember' our Galactic Family so we can be once again re- united with them. We will also re-discover our telepathic abilities once more. In fact, to really understand the potential that awaits us, you need only look at all the abilities that all the Masters that have come to this planet display, and all the abilities demonstrated by the Shaman of indigenous tribal cultures... this is our heritage! We are all Masters that have forgotten who we are!

The completion of this incredible quantum leap into a new dimension of consciousness is given as the year 2012/13. This corresponds to powerful astrological alignments and is also the point where our Star System will become fully immersed in the 'Photon-Band' (light particles discovered by Scientists in the 1960's). Various sources indicate that we will be immersed in this band of light for the next 2,600 years (approximately). Truly this will become the Age of Light. We can prepare here and NOW for this wonderful new 'dimension' to our reality, by embracing the concept of multi-dimensionality as a reality and live it in the NOW, choosing to see the Divine within *all things,* including one self. We will then see the return of the Wizards, Priestesses and benevolent Magic will once again turn this place into a wonderland.

This book now concludes at the beginning of the year 2006. To celebrate my awareness of our Star ancestry and the great adventure before us, I have completed a brand new *Elfin Spiral* album entitled *Pleiadean Love Dance* and I invite you all to join in with the dance! I have now reached a point in my life, where I truly thank the 'all that is' for the gift of life. I am in appreciation of all the wonderful gifts of wisdom that life has bestowed upon me. It has now become my priority to maintain my state of well-being, because from this, all else is reflected and created. It is therefore the greatest gift I can give my children and those that I love. It is only by being true to one self that we can be true to others.

Look at the story of 'YOUR LIFE' and review the guidance received within...

***Become the light of your own STAR***
***The STAR of your own life***
***A STAR being a STAR-BEING!...***

***BE THE STAR THAT YOU ARE!***

## *About the Author*

**Nick Ashron - Psychic Artist and
Visionary Musician**

Nick Ashron is a Psychic Artist and
Musician who is fast gaining
recognition in the 'Spiritual' arena
having featured frequently in 'New
Age' magazines and on television.

Nick Ashron started his career as a Portrait Artist in UK holiday
camps in 1971. His artistic skills eventually led him into drawing
Visionary Artwork and then on to the development of his skill for
channelling and drawing Spirit Guides. He is a regular attendee
of Psychic and Holistic Fayres in the UK and abroad, where he
works as a Psychic Artist.

After developing his own ability as a Healer in 1973, Nick came
to recognise that music is a powerful medium to transmit healing
energy, and Nick has been creating Inspirational Music for
healing and self-empowerment since 1975. His first band
*Pegasus* performed at one of the first ever *Mind Body Spirit*
events in Earls Court, London. He has now produced 10 albums
under his own record labels; *Wandering Minstrel Music* and *Star-
Ship Pegasus Promotions*. His band *Elfin Spiral* has been
gaining wide spread popularity both in the UK and the USA since
their first performance at the infamous Glastonbury Festival in
1995.

Nick has now ventured into writing with this, his first book, in the
hope of inspiring others in their own Spiritual journey.

For more information on Nick's Art, Music and Spirit Guide
Drawings - visit **www.nickashron.com**.

## Recommended Reading

Nick Ashron recommends the following books for further reading.*

*Bringers of the Dawn: Teachings from the Pleiadians*
Barbara Marciniak - Bear & Company
*Legends of the Star Ancestors: Stories of Extraterrestrial Contact from Wisdomkeepers Around the World*
Nancy Red Star - Bear & Company
*ET 101: The Cosmic Instruction Manual*
Zoev Jho, Diana Luppi and Mission Control - Godsfield Press Ltd
*The KRYON Series*
Lee Carroll - Kryon Writings,US
*The Ptaah Tapes: Transformation of the Species*
Jani King - Charles T. Banford Company
*Arcturians (Arcturian Star Chronicles)*
Patricia Pereira - Beyond Words Publishing
*Prism of Lyra: An Exploration of Human Galactic Heritage*
Lyssa Royal - Light Technology Publications
*The Only Planet of Choice: Essential Briefings from Deep Space*
Phyllis V. Schlemmer - Gateway
*The Arcturus Probe: Tales and Reports of an Ongoing Investigation*
Jose Arguelles - Windrush Publishing Services
*The Celestine Prophecy*
James Redfield - Bantam
*Conversations with God Series*
Neale Donald Walsch - Hodder & Stoughton Ltd
*Bridge Across Forever*
Richard Bach (Author of *Jonathan Livingston Seagull: A Story*) - Pan

*Authors Note: The recommendation of these books does not necessarily mean that I endorse every single word in them. Take, as I did, those things that resonate with you and put them to the test. Your own personal experiences will be your validation.

Also available from Real2Can
Books/Audio Books
Music
Films

www.real2can.com